# DEADLY DISEASES AND EPIDEMICS

# AVIAN FLU

Anthrax

Avian Flu

Botulism

Campylobacteriosis

Cholera

Ebola

Encephalitis

*Escherichia coli* Infections

Gonorrhea

Hantavirus Pulmonary Syndrome

Hepatitis

Herpes

HIV/AIDS

Infectious Fungi

Influenza

Legionnaires' Disease

Leprosy

Lyme Disease

Mad Cow Disease (Bovine Spongiform Encephalopathy)

Malaria

Meningitis

Mononucleosis

Pelvic Inflammatory Disease

Plague

Polio

*Salmonella*

SARS

Smallpox

*Streptococcus* (Group A)

*Staphylococcus aureus* Infections

Syphilis

Toxic Shock Syndrome

Tuberculosis

Tularemia

Typhoid Fever

West Nile Virus

# DEADLY DISEASES AND EPIDEMICS

# AVIAN FLU

## Jeffrey N. Sfakianos

FOUNDING EDITOR
The Late **I. Edward Alcamo**
Distinguished Teaching Professor of Microbiology,
SUNY Farmingdale

FOREWORD BY
**David Heymann**
World Health Organization

**CHELSEA HOUSE**
PUBLISHERS
An imprint of Infobase Publishing

Avian Flu

Chelsea House
An imprint of Infobase Publishing
132 West 31st Street
New York NY 10001

**Library of Congress Cataloging-in-Publication Data**

Sfakianos, Jeffrey N.
  Avian flu/Jeff Sfakianos.
    p. cm.—(Deadly diseases and epidemics)
  Includes bibliographical references.
ISBN 0-7910-8675-5
  1. Avian influenza—Juvenile literature. I. Title. II. Series.
RA644.I6S453 2005
614.5'18—dc22                                      2005021240

Chelsea House books are available at special discounts when purchased in bulk quantities for businesses, associations, institutions, or sales promotions. Please call our Special Sales Department in New York at (212) 967-8800 or (800) 322-8755.

You can find Chelsea House on the World Wide Web at http://www.chelseahouse.com

Series design by Terry Mallon
Cover design by Keith Trego

Printed in the United States of America

Bang 21C 10 9 8 7 6 5 4 3 2 1

This book is printed on acid-free paper.

All links and web addresses were checked and verified to be correct at the time of publication. Because of the dynamic nature of the web, some addresses and links may have changed since publication and may no longer be valid.

# Table of Contents

# Foreword

In the 1960s, many of the infectious diseases that had terrorized generations were tamed. After a century of advances, the leading killers of Americans both young and old were being prevented with new vaccines or cured with new medicines. The risk of death from pneumonia, tuberculosis (TB), meningitis, influenza, whooping cough, and diphtheria declined dramatically. New vaccines lifted the fear that summer would bring polio, and a global campaign was on the verge of eradicating smallpox worldwide. New pesticides like DDT cleared mosquitoes from homes and fields, thus reducing the incidence of malaria, which was present in the southern United States and which remains a leading killer of children worldwide. New technologies produced safe drinking water and removed the risk of cholera and other waterborne diseases. Science seemed unstoppable. Disease seemed destined to all but disappear.

But the euphoria of the 1960s has evaporated.

The microbes fought back. Those causing diseases like TB and malaria evolved resistance to cheap and effective drugs. The mosquito developed the ability to defuse pesticides. New diseases emerged, including AIDS, Legionnaires' disease, and Lyme disease. And diseases that had not been seen in decades re-emerged, as the hantavirus did in the Navajo Nation in 1993. Technology itself actually created new health risks. The global transportation network, for example, meant that diseases like West Nile virus could spread beyond isolated regions and quickly become global threats. Even modern public health protections sometimes failed, as they did in 1993 in Milwaukee, Wisconsin, resulting in 400,000 cases of the digestive system illness cryptosporidiosis. And, more recently, the threat from smallpox, a disease believed to be completely eradicated, has returned along with other potential bioterrorism weapons such as anthrax.

The lesson is that the fight against infectious diseases will never end.

In our constant struggle against disease, we as individuals have a weapon that does not require vaccines or drugs, and that is the warehouse of knowledge. We learn from the history of science that "modern" beliefs can be wrong. In this series of books, for example, you will learn that diseases like syphilis were once thought to be caused by eating potatoes. The invention of the microscope set science on the right path. There are more positive lessons from history. For example, smallpox was eliminated by vaccinating everyone who had come in contact with an infected person. This "ring" approach to smallpox control is still the preferred method for confronting an outbreak, should the disease be intentionally reintroduced.

At the same time, we are constantly adding new drugs, new vaccines, and new information to the warehouse. Recently, the entire human genome was decoded. So too was the genome of the parasite that causes malaria. Perhaps by looking at the microbe and the victim through the lens of genetics we will be able to discover new ways to fight malaria, which remains the leading killer of children in many countries.

Because of advances in our understanding of such diseases as AIDS, entire new classes of antiretroviral drugs have been developed. But resistance to all these drugs has already been detected, so we know that AIDS drug development must continue.

Education, experimentation, and the discoveries that grow out of them are the best tools to protect health. Opening this book may put you on the path of discovery. I hope so, because new vaccines, new antibiotics, new technologies, and, most importantly, new scientists are needed now more than ever if we are to remain on the winning side of this struggle against microbes.

David Heymann
Executive Director
Communicable Diseases Section
World Health Organization
Geneva, Switzerland

# 1

# Introduction

## SEARCHING FOR A DEADLY DISEASE

In 1918, cities and towns across the United States were under **quarantine**. The country, and most of the world, was living in fear of an invisible enemy that was rumored to destroy everything in its path. Brevig, Alaska was one such town. Brevig's 80 citizens did not leave the town for fear of encountering the enemy, and outsiders were not allowed in the small town for fear that they may bring the enemy with them. Despite all of Brevig's fear and efforts to quarantine the townspeople, the enemy did find its way inside the town. A cargo ship was allowed to dock on Alaska's shores after it was mistakenly determined to be free of harm. Among the ship's cargo was a bag of letters for the citizens of Brevig and a few other Alaskan towns. The local letter carrier picked up the bag with his dogsled team shortly after the ship docked at the port. Soon after, the carrier began his journey to deliver the letters to the nearby towns. The morning that the man began his carrier route, he was not sick, but he rapidly became ill during his journey. The disease that caused his sickness was the enemy that held the world hostage and it rapidly attacked his lungs. The disease caused him to drown in his own blood by the end of the day. Less than 12 hours after he had started his journey, the letter carrier lay dead, bent over the harness of his sled. The dogs that were pulling his sled realized that their leader had died and loyally directed the sled toward his home town of Brevig. A friend saw the dogs approaching and rushed out to meet the sled. After realizing that the man was unconscious, others quickly came to help. Unfortunately, the goodwill of the townspeople had allowed the enemy to enter every home of Brevig, Alaska. All of Brevig's residents, except for eight children, died within 4 days.

Nearly 80 years later, in the frozen landscapes of Alaska, a team of scientists worked through harsh conditions in search of the graves of the citizens of Brevig. If the scientists succeeded in their quest, they would retrieve the world's only sample of the pathogen that caused the most horrific disease humanity has ever experienced. The team used a sophisticated instrument designed to survey structures beneath the frozen ground. The instrument emitted ground-penetrating radar signals that bounced back signals to reveal frozen forms resting deep beneath the surface. On that day, the team had successfully used the radar to identify the graveyard that likely held the population of the town of Brevig. Tombstones on the surface, not far from the site where the coffins were identified, indicated that people were buried at this location in the year 1918. That all of the 72 people buried at this location died of natural causes at the same time was highly unlikely. Additionally, historical records indicated that a graveyard had been created in this vicinity to bury the diseased victims. Thus, it was a strong possibility that the bodies inside the coffins were Brevig's victims of the virus that caused the greatest influenza **pandemic** that the world has ever known. The virus became known as the 1918 Spanish flu. This was because Spain had remained neutral during World War I, which was occurring at the same time that the influenza virus was ravaging the world, and Spain gave the virus more public attention than any other country. It was hoped that the frozen ground, which would have preserved the bodies in the grave, would also have preserved the disease that was responsible for their deaths. However, the frozen ground, combined with the contents of the coffins, required that the team's digging tools be driven as accurately as they were forcefully. If one of the shovels were to strike a coffin and break the enclosure, then the team risked releasing this deadly disease again.

What the team sought was the **influenza virus** that caused the flu during the disease outbreak in Brevig. To say that the

1918 flu season was particularly bad would most definitely be an understatement. The virus that circulated during that year, and the subsequent year, killed more people than have been killed in any of the world's wars. The virus spread around the world in a matter of months. An alarming characteristic of the virus was that it targeted a population unlike any other disease. The target was not the weakened immune systems of the young and the old, but instead the most common victims were healthy adults. Infection could progress so rapidly that the victims drowned in their own blood mere hours after the symptoms had become apparent. The severity of the infection and the fact that the victim represented the backbone of productive society combined to ensure the world was deeply and devastatingly afflicted by the disease. By the time the pandemic had subsided, an estimated 50 million people had succumbed to the Spanish flu's wrath (Figure 1.1).

Unfortunately, very little was known about viruses in 1918. At the time of the Spanish flu outbreak, most physicians thought the **pathogen**, which was killing millions of people, was caused by a **bacterium** instead of a virus. However, the disease killed its victims so rapidly—and physicians's fear of catching the disease was so great—that medical studies on the pathogen were limited. As a result, no samples of the Spanish flu pathogen were isolated and very little is known regarding why this particular virus was so much more deadly than other flu viruses. The scientists that were exhuming the frozen bodies from the coffins hoped that the 1918 influenza virus had been preserved by the subzero temperatures. If a sample of the virus could be obtained from the bodies, the pathogen could be studied in a scientific laboratory. Ultimately, the scientists hoped that a sample of the virus could answer questions about the unusual severity of the disease. Reports of this virus were unlike any other that had been recorded before, and many experts predict that a similar influenza virus that emerged in Asia in the late 1990s may

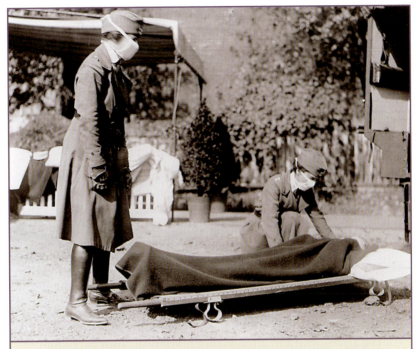

**Figure 1.1** Two emergency workers demonstrate how to care for an influenza patient at a Red Cross Emergency Ambulance Station in 1918.

soon produce a terror on the world similar to that produced by the 1918 Spanish flu.

## SUBSEQUENT OUTBREAKS OF INFLUENZA

Since the horrific 1918 flu outbreak, two more outbreaks have caused deadly pandemics but have been less severe than the Spanish flu outbreak. The first of these outbreaks occurred in 1957 and was called the Asian flu since it was discovered in China. Overall, the virus killed an estimated 1 million people worldwide; approximately 70,000 of those killed were Americans. Another outbreak, known as the Hong Kong flu, followed in 1968 and killed an estimated 500,000 people. This virus also reached the United States and caused the death of approximately 34,000 Americans. Both of these viruses seemed to have the normal inclination toward its range of victims compared with other known flu viruses (Figure 1.2). That is, they both targeted the weak **immune systems** of young children and the elderly, in contrast to the Spanish flu, which primarily targeted healthy adults. In fact, it is thought that children helped to facilitate the spread of these viruses, and other yearly flu outbreaks, through everyday contacts with one another at school. This tendency of the virus to attack individuals with weaker immune systems allows most healthy adults to resist fatal illness after being infected. This trait is mainly due to a person's ability to fight the virus and clear it from the body before it causes a disease.

Doomsayers have been predicting an upcoming flu season that may be as vicious as the one in 1918. The predictions are based on knowledge of influenza virus cycles and the mutations that occur in the virus with every flu season, which will be discussed in later chapters. Scientists who study the influenza virus have realized that the virus mutates each season. These season-to-season mutations are relatively harmless, creating a virus that is slightly different but no more deadly than the virus of the prior season. However, these scientists are especially alarmed that the virus seems to undergo a drastic change every 30 years, a cycle that results in a mutated virus that becomes far more deadly than the viruses of the previous years. Thus far, this predicted trend has held true. The world has seen three deadly outbreaks in the last century. A fourth outbreak may be just over the horizon. Thus, there is an urgency to understanding how the previous three flu viruses became so deadly, and from where these deadly viruses emerged.

Ultimately, a sample of the Spanish flu virus of 1918 was extracted from one of the bodies in the grave of Brevig, Alaska and another from a similar grave site of a Norwegian town. Studies on these 1918 viruses and the related flu viruses of

# Past flu pandemics

There were three influenza pandemics – global outbreaks of the disease – during the 20th century, killing hundreds of thousands of people in the United States and millions worldwide.

## Approximate number of deaths in the United States

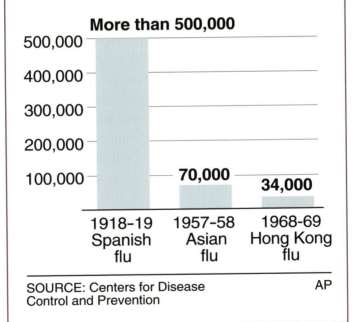

SOURCE: Centers for Disease Control and Prevention                                    AP

**Figure 1.2** The Spanish flu, Asian flu, and Hong Kong flu were three pandemics that erupted in the 20th century, which combined to kill more than 600,000 Americans.

1957 and 1968 revealed that these viruses were more closely related to bird influenza viruses than to the influenza viruses that normally targeted humans. Moreover, it was found that although these viruses were most likely derived from a bird virus, they could be efficiently transmitted from human to human. Thus, three conditions separated these deadly viruses from other less deadly flu viruses. First, each virus was new to the human population. **Immunity** had not been established and **vaccines**, if available at all, were not effective against the viruses, so very little resistance was met as the virus spread through the human population. Second, the viruses were able to replicate in humans and manifest a disease. The three deadly viruses caused severe respiratory distress in their victims, which frequently led to death in the infected person. Third and most critical, these deadly viruses could be transmitted from person to person. This third condition is critical because it allows the viruses, which would be otherwise geographically isolated by ecological niches, to spread throughout the world. The flu viruses that emerge year after year in the human population are generally only slightly different from the virus that was circulated the previous year. Thus, in most cases, circulating human flu viruses meet the third criteria but are neither new to the human population nor are able to evade the available vaccines.

## THE NEXT PANDEMIC?

The three conditions discussed in the previous section were satisfied by transmission of a flu virus from the avian, or bird, population to the human population, resulting in an infectious disease. Scientists of the World Health Organization (WHO) and the Centers for Disease Control and Prevention (CDC) are extremely concerned that these conditions may again be emerging. A new flu virus was discovered in Asia during the 1997 flu season. This new virus has already duplicated the first two conditions that could lead to a deadly pandemic of the flu. The new virus emerged from an avian flu virus that is currently prevalent in Asian waterfowl and, since 2004, has been transmitted to a reported 58 humans, 18 of whom died of severe respiratory disease. These cases were limited to Asian cities. The strain of the virus that infected these people was found to be similar to a virus that has been circulating in the

## DEATHS FROM INFLUENZA

Nearly every year in the United States, epidemics of influenza occur during the winter months. The disease is caused by a virus, the influenza type A virus, that changes every year. The continual changes usually result in evasions of the immune system. Thus, complete immunity to the virus is difficult to achieve, but resistance to disease can be developed. Influenza infects hundreds of thousands of people every year and results in a staggering 20,000 deaths per year in the United States alone. The virus infects children at the highest rates, but causes the most severe disease in people above the age of 65 years. The disease usually results in respiratory complications, fever, headache, sore throat, cough, and body aches. These symptoms can persist for 2 or more weeks, but typically resolve after several days. This may seem like a large burden to deal with every flu season, but the numbers are predicted to be much higher if the circulating influenza virus undergoes an abrupt change in its composition. Periodically, the prevailing human strain of influenza undergoes a large change that results in a virus that is not recognized by the immune system. This virus may replicate in the body without disruption by the host's defense system. The disease that results from such an abrupt change can cause deaths in the tens of millions. The threat of staggering death tolls around the world from the emergence of a new virus that could reach the human population currently has the world health organizations on high alert.

bird population, but that had not been observed in humans before 1997. Thus, the virus satisfied condition number one since it was new to humans and current vaccines could not effectively generate immunity to the virus. Additionally, the virus caused respiratory disease in many of the people that were infected, causing fatalities in one-third of those victims, which satisfies condition number two. Currently, there is limited evidence that the new virus can be transmitted from person to person. A few stories of isolated cases provide the only evidence that the third condition has been met. One such case was identified in Thailand during the 2004 flu season. A mother likely became infected with the flu virus from her daughter, who possibly became infected at work. These stories fail to provide conclusive evidence that the virus is beginning to satisfy the person-to-person transmission characteristics of a deadly pandemic flu virus, but they are more than enough to catch the attention of international health officials.

The new avian flu virus that has emerged in Asia has acquired the ability to infect humans with deadly results. If this virus mutates further, the virus may acquire the ability to be transmitted from person to person. Thus this avian virus has the potential to be the cause of the next deadly flu pandemic. The WHO and the CDC are desperately trying to monitor this virus and ensure that affected countries have the ability to combat this disease before it spreads around the world.

# 2

# The Avian Influenza Virus

## WHAT ARE VIRUSES?

Viruses, extremely small particles that are neither dead nor alive, were first predicted to exist in the mid-1800s. The prediction was made by a German scientist, Jacob Henle, who studied anatomy. Dr. Henle postulated that infectious particles existed that were too small to be visualized through a light microscope. Unfortunately, convincing the world that something exists but is too small to be seen is not easy. A series of historic discoveries and experiments eventually proved Dr. Henle's concepts to be true. However, it is ironic that the breakthroughs that lead to belief in the concept of viruses came from the inability of viruses to adhere to three determinants of a disease-causing agent.

The first of the determinants was pioneered by Louis Pasteur, whose experimentation disproved the concept of **spontaneous generation**. Dr. Pasteur incorporated flasks that had a shape like a swan's neck. He could place a **fermentable** "juice" in the flasks and sterilize the solution. As long as the flasks were kept closed or only exposed to air through the curved neck of the flask, which prevented dust in the air from reaching the juice, the liquid remained sterile (Figure 2.1). The indication of sterility in his experiment was actually the lack of growth in his nutrient-rich juice. However, if dust or contaminated water was allowed to touch the juice, then the solution itself became contaminated, and **microorganisms** made the juice putrid. The concept of the experiment was simple. If microorganisms could be spontaneously generated out of the air, then the juice would become putrid without touching dust or some other source of contamination. Alternatively (and what we know to be true today), if microorganisms come from parent microorganisms, then the juice

**Figure 2.1** A swan-neck flask such as this one was used by Louis Pasteur to disprove the theory of spontaneous generation. The experiment led to the establishment of Koch's postulates.

must be seeded with a contaminant that grows and replicates in the nutrients of the juice. The results made a huge impact around the world. Not only did the results disprove the theory of spontaneous generation, but they started the technique of **pasteurization** (heating a solution to kill all of the microorganisms). As long as a solution was pasteurized, it did not become contaminated with microbes. Furthermore, when different sources were used to inoculate the juice, different effects of fermentation were observed. This led to the concept that different microbes existed with different biological properties.

A young student of Dr. Henle named Robert Koch (Figure 2.2) extended the concept of uniquely different microorganisms by discovering that two different germs cause distinctly different diseases in humans. Effectively, an infection by one type of microorganism may cause a similar disease in many different people and that another type of germ would be the cause if a group of people developed a disease with different symptoms. Although the concept of this discovery seems simple to us today, it actually set the foundation for many groundbreaking discoveries that rapidly followed. A third scientist, Joseph Lister, along with Dr. Koch learned how to isolate individual germs using dilutions and gelatins to grow the individual germs into populations that could be easily managed and studied under a light microscope. These techniques, developed in the late 1800s, became the standards of medical science and are still used in some laboratories today.

The work of Louis Pasteur, Robert Koch, and Joseph Lister were eventually formulated into a set of rules that a microorganism must adhere to if it was to be defined as the causative agent of a disease. These rules are referred to as **Koch's postulates**. Koch's postulates require that 1) the suspected microorganism must be strongly associated with the disease, 2) the microorganism must be isolated and grown outside of the host, 3) transfer of the microorganism to an uninfected host must cause the disease in that host, and 4) the microorganism must be re-isolated from the new host and cause the

**Figure 2.2** Robert Koch working at his laboratory bench. Viruses initially evaded Koch's postulates partially because of the technology that was available to scientists at the time.

same disease. Koch's postulates held true for some diseases. For example, Koch used these postulates to discover a deadly microorganism known as ***Bacillus anthracis*** in rabbits. As the postulates require, Koch isolated *Bacillus anthracis* from rabbits that had the symptoms of an anthrax infection. Then he infected healthy rabbits with the purified cultures and watched as the rabbits developed the disease. To satisfy the final criteria, *Bacillus anthracis* was isolated from the newly infected rabbits. Using Koch's postulates, it was discovered that the microorganism that caused the disease known as anthrax was in fact *Bacillus anthracis*.

Fortunately for Dr. Jacob Henle's reputation, Koch's postulates could not always be applied. Due to a lack of advanced techniques available to scientists at the time the postulates were developed, Koch's postulates could not account for diseases caused by **obligatory pathogens**. Obligatory pathogens cannot survive on the nutrients available in the rich broths, juices, or gelatins that were used to isolate microorganisms such as *Bacillus anthracis*. Instead, obligatory pathogens require a host cell that they can infect and replicate within. Although obligatory pathogens are routinely isolated today by using a broth or gelatin containing host cells for the pathogens to use, the culture mediums of the late 1800s could not culture every disease-causing agent. Therefore, Henle's prediction of a submicroscopic organism was still unaccounted for, but also could not be ruled out. Some diseases could not be isolated and propagated into pure populations, but could be transferred from host to host. Furthermore, these pathogens could cause a disease in the new host. Thus the concept of a "virus" was beginning to evolve, although the concept was primarily founded in an inability to define a pathogen.

A second experimental description of this underdescribed phenomenon was that the disease-causing agent was very small. The agent was actually so small that the available filters of the time could not remove the cause of disease from the solution. Filters were generally used to trap microorganisms that could subsequently generate more microorganisms when placed in a suitable broth. However, some disease-causing agents remained in the liquid phase of the filtrate. Using *Bacillus anthracis* as an example again, this microorganism could be collected in a large volume of saline by washing a wound from an infected rabbit. This wash fluid containing *Bacillus anthracis* from the wound could then be passed through a filter. The *Bacillus anthracis* would then be scraped off the top of the filter, grown in a broth, and used to infect other rabbits, causing disease in each of these rabbits. However, and most importantly to Dr. Henle, the liquid that flowed through the filter was effectively sterilized, as it was free of any disease-causing agent. This result was the direct effect of the microorganism's size, which was too large to pass through the small pores of the filter. Dr. Henle had predicted the existence of a submicroscopic organism that was too small to be caught by a filter. The first evidence of such an organism was becoming apparent. Several scientists had found that some diseases could not be removed from liquid solutions by filtration. Thus, the still unproven existence of "viruses" gained a second descriptive term based on their small size. The inability to filter out the infectious agent became the second indication of the existence of a virus.

Eventually, a Dutch scientist described a "living liquid" that could be diluted and then regain its strength when grown in cultured, living tissues. This was the first indication of an organism that could not be seen through a light microscope and could not be filtered out of a liquid, yet could replicate itself under the right conditions. The description was extended to show that the liquid containing the agent was also contagious. That is, the living liquid was filtered, strengthened in living tissue, and then used to infect other specimens. Since this work was actually performed with the virus that is known today as tobacco mosaic virus, there was still some skepticism that the same concepts could be observed for animals. After all, the tobacco mosaic virus only caused disease in tobacco plants (Figure 2.3). Although this work had great implications for the diseases of plants, the intellectual link between plants

**Figure 2.3** The study of the tobacco mosaic virus helped scientists to understand the properties of viruses and bacteria. This leaf is displaying the effects of the virus (white spots).

and animals was still very distant. The information gained from studies with the tobacco mosaic virus led to the identification and description of one of the first viruses discovered to infect humans, yellow fever virus. This virus was described in 1901 by Walter Reed.

At the turn of the 20th century, the world's scientists had become aware of a new organism that could cause disease in a wide range of specimens, including bacteria, plants, and animals. Viruses were primarily described by their small size and parasitic nature.

## THE STRUCTURE OF VIRUSES

As knowledge of viruses progressed from a concept to an experimentally defined disease-causing agent, scientists struggled to categorize the vast diversity of viruses being identified. This included arguments over some fundamental questions about viruses, such as whether they were animal or plant in nature. An enormous boost to the study of animal viruses was created through the independent work of several American scientists. These scientists developed techniques that allowed animal cells to be cultured in test tubes. This method of growing single cells in a dish and incubator under precise conditions became known as tissue culture. The boost to the study of viruses was that studies similar to those using tobacco mosaic virus in plant tissues could now be performed with animal viruses. With this technique, scientists possessed the tools to conduct experiments that revealed the secrets of animal viruses.

The study of viruses in tissue cultures revealed that the simplest description of a virus is a capsule used for the transfer of genetic material between living cells. A virus possesses all of the machinery necessary to direct its replication in a cell, package genetic material into a protective shell, and then transfer this material to another cell. The process is self-perpetuating through a general replication cycle that is common among all viruses. This replication cycle involves first allowing the capsule to attach to and enter a target cell. Inside the cell the virus begins replicating its genetic material and producing new shells in which it will package the replication products. The newly created capsules must also devise the manner in which it will leave the cell. Variations in this simplistic replication cycle have produced viruses that can infect every species of bacteria, plant, and animal. Additionally, inherent errors in the replication cycle continue to produce greater diversity among the species through **mutagenesis**, which generates the spontaneous changes in the virus.

The details of the replication cycle are only beginning to be discovered by the scientists who study viruses. Interestingly, hindsight has revealed that the details of the efficient nature of the virus are beautifully reflected in its structure. Above all else, the structure of the virus is designed to protect the genetic material that it carries. The largest portion of the virus's structure is, in fact, dedicated to this role. The tightly packaged genetic material is carefully packaged into a protein shell. The shell is often referred to as a **capsid** or coat and generates the scaffold for the virus shape. The material that makes the capsid can be visualized through an **electron microscope** as a dense sphere. The capsid is enveloped by a fatty layer that prevents smaller molecules from getting into the virus and also prevents the genetic material from leaving the virus. The fatty layer, or lipid layer, functions like an oil droplet. The lipid layer repels water from the virus and maintains an isolated environment for the contents within the virus.

Several proteins can also be visualized protruding outward from the virus. These projections reach out toward the environment and search for the virus's next target. Since these projections are often the target of the host's immune system, the projections are more frequently mutated than any other molecules on the virus. Subtle changes in the shape of the projections can effectively enable the virus to escape from the body's defense system. However, the amount of change that can be tolerated is limited. The projections must maintain the ability to find the next target and to mediate the entry of the virus into this target. Once inside the new target, the virus begins generating new viruses, and each of these viruses continues the replication cycle.

## IS THE AVIAN FLU SIMILAR TO OTHER VIRUSES?

The themes described above are only slightly varied for most viruses. The variation of different viruses is primarily derived from the differences in the species that the virus infects. Consistent with this, the avian influenza virus is very much like the viruses that have been described in the paragraphs above, but the avian influenza virus has become specialized to infect birds. The name *avian* is derived from the Latin word for bird, *avis*. The word *influenza*, or flu, comes from the disease that the virus causes, a viral disease that usually affects the respiratory tract. Like humans, young birds often become very sick and die from virus infections. Therefore, the avian influenza virus is simply the virus that causes flu in birds. Avian viruses, similar to human viruses, are contagious and periodically circulate among the host population. A single virus can be transmitted from bird to bird, and may cause a large amount of damage if the virus infects a farm that grows birds and keeps the birds in pens where they are often excessively close to one another.

Avian influenza viruses are very similar to the flu viruses that infect humans and circulate every year in the United States as well as in other countries around the world. In fact, the avian flu viruses and the influenza viruses that infect humans are actually in the same family of viruses and probably evolved from a common ancestor. So does this mean that birds also "catch the flu" like people? They certainly do! In fact, the bird flu caused by avian influenza is very similar to the flu that humans suffer. The similarities are that the severity of the symptoms varies between birds, and also varies from season to season. For wild birds, infections by the flu virus are usually not deadly. However, domesticated birds, such as ducks, turkeys, and chickens that are raised for consumption can become very sick from the infection, causing economic hardship for the poultry industry. The greater susceptibility of domesticated birds to the virus is not generally understood, but may be the result of genetic differences in breeding stocks or the "lifestyle" of domesticated birds versus that of wild birds.

The striking similarities of the avian and human influenza viruses have also caused fear beyond the loss of poultry. In fact, the avian influenza virus has become the number one concern of the World Health Organization, which primarily concerns itself with human health. This fear extends from the fact that the avian flu virus is normally, but not always, restricted to birds. The deadly influenza pandemics that killed millions of people during the 20th century were the result of an avian flu virus that gained the uncommon ability to infect humans. When the virus leaps the boundaries between species, the results can be deadly. On the rare occasion that a virus

## DETERMINING THE STRUCTURES OF VIRUSES

The technologies available for scientists to study the structures of biological specimens are far superior to the microscopes used by Henle, Pasteur, Lister, and Koch. Today, virus preparations can be rapidly frozen in an aqueous solution, which prevents ice crystals from forming around the specimen. The frozen objects can subsequently be viewed under an electron microscope without staining or further manipulating the samples. This technique can be automated so that hundreds of specimens can be analyzed during the experiment. The structures viewed under the microscope are then arranged and averaged using a computer. The result is a three-dimensional model of a virus. Another technique for virus visualization is scanning electron microscopy. This type of microscopy fires a beam of electrons at a fixed specimen that has been coated with a heavy metal. The metal causes many of the electrons to be reflected from the object and collected on a detector. The results of a scanning electron microscope produce a high resolution scan of the surface of a specimen.

mutates to gain the ability to cross the species barrier, the first two conditions that favor a deadly pandemic have been met: the virus is new to the accepting species and the virus causes a disease in that species. Meeting the last condition requires further mutation to allow the new virus to be transmitted among the new species. Thus, under normal conditions, a virus is rarely transmitted between species. Furthermore, when the virus is transmitted between species, the virus usually will not spread. It requires two consecutive unlikely mutations to favor a deadly pandemic. Unfortunately, a strain of avian flu has recently emerged in Asia that has gained the ability to infect humans. Not unexpectedly, the humans that were infected died from the disease caused by the viral infection. If the virus mutates further and gains the capacity for human-to-human transmission, then another deadly pandemic may strike the world.

# 3

# Molecular Structure of the Avian Influenza Virus

During the early 1900s, viruses were characterized based on the ability of the virus to infect animal, plant, or bacterial cells and on the size of the virus particle. Viruses could be separated from most other infectious microorganisms by passing the solution containing the virus through a filter. As filtration technologies advanced, the diameter of **virions** could be estimated by determining the smallest filter pore size that failed to remove the virus from a solution. Detection of the virus in the filtrate was primarily determined by the solution's ability to infect cells after being passed through the filter. If the solution remained infectious after filtration, then the virus was smaller than that pore size. If the solution lost the ability to infect cells after filtration, then the virus was trapped in the filter and some conclusions regarding the relative size of the virus could be made by comparing it to the pore size of the filter that was used. Today, it is understood that virions can take on many different shapes and sizes. Viruses can be spherical, icosahedral, or helical, and each of these different shapes may vary in size, commonly between 75 and 200 nanometers (Figure 3.1). Evolution of virus families has restricted specific viruses to form only one of the shapes. The restriction to one particular shape likely conveys specific advantages to the virus during the virus replication cycle. For instance, the human immunodeficiency virus (HIV) takes on a spherical form that could help the virus enter its next host cell by allowing proteins to freely move around on the surface of the viral envelope. After the virus attaches to the cell surface, the gp120 and gp41 proteins could concentrate on one side of

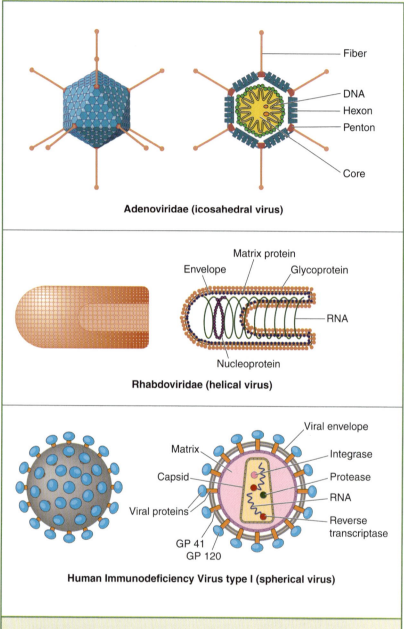

**Figure 3.1** Viruses come in a variety of shapes, including icosahedral, helical, and spherical, which are illustrated here.

the spherical virus and work together to promote entry into the cell. Similarly, helical shapes likely ease entry of the rhabdoviruses into a target cell. These viruses enter a cell by a mechanism called endocytosis. This cellular process involves active engulfing of various particles into the cell. However, the size of particles engulfed by this process are restricted in diameter, but not in length. Thus, the helical rhabdovirus has evolved a long thin form that allows the virus to take advantage of this natural cellular process to gain entry into the cell. The icosahedral shape of the adenovirus also conveys advantages to the virus. The shape of the virus is formed by only a limited number of different protein molecules. The molecules are arranged into units of hexamers (6-sided shapes). These hexamers are ordered to form a larger triangle, which comes together around a pentameric (5-sided) vertex. The resulting assembly of the triangles around the pentameric vertex is an icosahedral shape that is extremely stable and capable of withstanding harsh conditions inside and outside of the body. Each of these shapes can vary in size. The size of the virus is dictated by the size of the virus genome. To accommodate larger genomes a helical virus grows longer, an icosahedral virus assembles larger triangles, and a spherical virus forms larger spheres. Furthermore, despite understanding much more about the general nature of viruses, such as the nature of the genetic material that is packaged into the virus and the host that the virus prefers to replicate in, size and shape still remain the primary characteristics that are used to categorize viruses. Advances in molecular biology have allowed the molecular structure of viruses to be included in this classification with greater detail than could have been imagined when Koch's postulates were first identified in the late nineteenth century.

In the case of avian influenza viruses, the virions are spherical with a diameter of 80 to 120 nanometers. As with all viruses, the structures of the spherical particles are composed of only a few different molecules that can be categorized as capsid proteins, **glycoproteins**, and the genetic material. All of these molecules work together to orchestrate the various stages of the virus replication cycle. The capsid proteins bind to the genetic material, which contains the identity of the virus, and the glycoproteins function to navigate the virus to and from different cells in the body infected by the virus. The genome of the avian influenza virus is encoded by eight separate strands of ribonucleic acid (RNA). Each of these strands encodes a different component of the avian influenza virus and is the source of variation for the virus (Figure 3.2). The avian influenza virus also possesses molecules derived from the host. Among the host-derived molecules is an encapsulation composed of a fatty coat and cholesterol, known as a lipid bilayer. The lipid bilayer is wrapped around the virion and generates a continuous barrier between the outside environment and the inside of the virus shell. These molecular features of the avian influenza viruses are common components of all influenza viruses. Furthermore, the variations in these components are the determinants of classification within the family of influenza viruses.

## CLASSIFICATION OF INFLUENZA VIRUSES

Fine variation in the influenza virus capsids, which wrap around the virus's genetic material, are initially used to classify the viruses into three broad types. These types are A, B, and C. Two specific components of the virus capsid, termed the nucleocapsid (NP) component and the matrix (M) component, are the primary determinants of which category the virus belongs in. The subtle differences in the two capsid components are based on recognition by parts of the host's immune system called **antibodies**. Antibodies are an integral part of the response that is launched by an organism after its body recognizes a foreign invader. Since the capsid

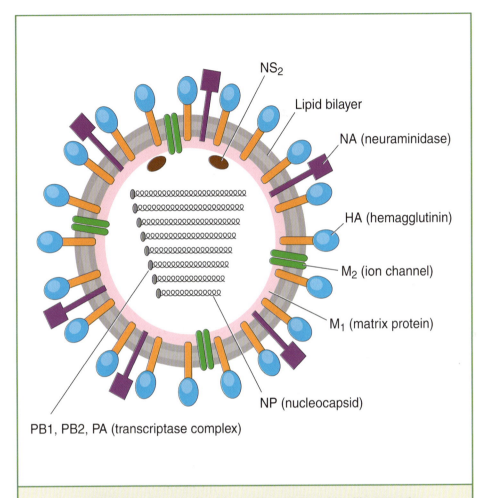

NS$_2$

Lipid bilayer

NA (neuraminidase)

HA (hemagglutinin)

M$_2$ (ion channel)

M$_1$ (matrix protein)

NP (nucleocapsid)

PB1, PB2, PA (transcriptase complex)

**Figure 3.2** The structure of an influenza virus virion illustrates the surface proteins, hemagglutinin, and neuraminidase. Additionally, the genetic material and other virus components can be visualized within the lipid membrane.

components that are used to classify the influenza viruses are not easily accessible by the antibodies, there is not a strong selective pressure on these components to change or mutate. Therefore, these components remain more stable in size and shape than some of the components that protrude outward from the virus and are easily accessible by the anti-bodies. The stability of these components in the face of an ever-changing virus makes them ideal for classifying the broad types (A, B, and C). Additionally, this classification of the virus family also relates other important information. Virus typing is a strong indicator of the range of species that the virus may target and may also indicate the severity of the disease caused by an infection. For example, the type C influenza viruses are primarily limited to humans, but have also been found to infect pigs. The type C influenza viruses only cause a mild disease in their hosts and have not ever been the source of a pandemic, or for that matter, an epidemic. The type B influenza virus is also found primarily in humans and has also not been the source of a pandemic. However, type B influenza viruses have occasionally been the source of epidemic diseases.

The influenza virus that has the broadest host range and is the source of all of the pandemics that have struck the world is the influenza type A virus. Influenza viruses of this type can infect humans, birds, pigs, horses, seals, and whales (Figure 3.3). Additionally, this type is the only virus that can routinely produce fatal diseases in its host. Although the type A influenza viruses do have a broad host range, the primary host is wild birds, in which the virus continuously circu-lates—primarily among populations of waterfowl. Inside the bird's body, the viruses rapidly evolve through the genera-tion and selection of mutations. This evolution comes from the rapid replication of the virus and the selective pressure of the **progeny** virus. An avian influenza virus could hypotheti-cally infect a cell within a bird and then produce daughter viruses that leave the cell within 6 hours. An interesting trait of avian influenza viruses and many viruses in general is the lack of fidelity that accompanies the viruses' rapid replica-tion cycle. When a virus infects a cell and begins copying itself, the copying machinery is error prone and the progeny

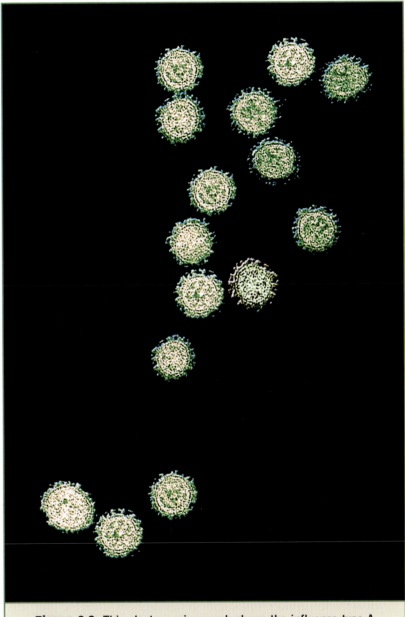

**Figure 3.3** This electron micrograph shows the influenza type A virus, magnified 62,500 times. Influenza of this type can infect humans, birds, pigs, horses, seals, and whales.

viruses always exhibit a slight variation from the parent
virus. Sometimes the variation is not tolerated by the virus,
and these viruses cannot completely function in subsequent
replication cycles. These disabling mutations can be thought
of as boundary-defining mutations. Changes that drive the
virus outside of its boundaries disrupt the ability of the virus
to successfully complete the replication cycle. However,
viruses frequently generate mutations within these boundaries; such mutations are tolerated by the replication cycle
and potentially have a variety of effects on the virus and the
disease it causes.

The direct result of tolerated mutations or changes in
the virus is the continued evasion of the host's immune system. The antibodies that are created by the immune system
recognize specific structures or shapes that are present on
the components of the virus, known as **epitopes.** Antibodies
are the primary defense against an avian influenza virus
infection and are capable of inactivating the virus when they
bind to these epitopes. The nature of the interaction between
antibodies and avian influenza virus will be discussed in
further detail in Chapter 6. However, what is important to
know for this chapter is that antibodies are very effective at
destroying a virus once the antibody binds to the virus. Two
important phenomena represent the cause and effect of this
interaction. As stated above, infidelity in the replication
cycle of the virus results in continuous changes in the epitopes of the virus. The changes to the virus can cause antibodies to fail to recognize the specific epitopes, thus allowing
these mutated viruses to evade destruction by the defense
system. The results are that viruses may avoid detection by
antibodies through mutagenesis. Avoidance of the immune
system by some viruses and destruction of other viruses
results in a selection of random mutants. This recognition
by antibodies and the destruction of viruses that fail to
avoid detection is known as **selective pressure.** The selective

pressure causes a phenomenon known as **antigenic drift**, which is the slow but persistent evolution of the avian influenza virus. In summary, mutation in the avian influenza virus causes diversity in the population of viruses, whereas selective pressure results in outgrowth of only the viruses that can avoid detection by antibodies.

The components of avian influenza virus that experience the greatest selective pressure are the glycoproteins that protrude from the virus shell. There are two such components on the avian influenza virus known as the **hemagglutinin** and the **neuraminidase** glycoproteins. Both of these glycoproteins have critical functions in directing the virus through the body, from the cell that produced the virus and towards the next cell that will be infected. However, since the glycoproteins are the outermost components of the virus, they are the easiest to detect by antibodies. Thus, unlike the matrix and nucleocapsid components mentioned above, the glycoproteins vary drastically among the broad types of influenza viruses. In fact, selective pressure on type A influenza viruses has generated 15 different types of hemagglutinin (HA or H) molecules and 9 different types of neuraminidase (NA or N) glycoproteins. These different HA and NA glycoproteins have been used to further categorize the type A influenza viruses into subtypes. The subtypes of type A influenza virus are named by the subtype number of hemagglutinin and neuraminidase using the single letter abbreviation and the number of the subtype. For example, the 1918 influenza virus that killed nearly 50 million people worldwide was subtyped as H1N1. The annotation "H1N1" means that this A type influenza virus possesses the subtype 1 hemagglutinin and the subtype 1 neuraminidase glycoproteins.

So what do the hemagglutinin and neuraminidase glycoproteins do? The hemagglutinin molecule is the major antigenic molecule of the virus. This means that the host's immune system usually identifies this molecule on the influenza virus before all others. Therefore, the hemagglutinin molecule has the greatest selective pressure and thus the greatest diversification among the influenza components. Despite having the most diversity among the influenza components, all of the type A influenza hemagglutinin molecules perform the same function. The hemagglutinin glycoprotein has the important role of mediating the attachment to the target cell, and also the entry of the virus into the target cell. The hemagglutinin glycoprotein performs these events by binding to a specific molecule on the surface of the target cells. Only the cells that express this molecule will be targeted by the virus for infection. Soon after attaching to the cell, the glycoprotein is induced to undergo a large change in shape, which exposes a part of the glycoprotein that was previously buried within the molecule. The newly exposed part of the hemagglutinin is called the fusion peptide and gets injected into the membrane of the target cell. After several of the virus hemagglutinin molecules insert fusion peptides into the target cell membrane, the virus lipid coat and the cell fuse to form one continuous membrane. Similar to when two drops of oil merge into a single droplet with a combined volume, the fusion of the cell and virus membranes results in the influenza capsid proteins and genetic material moving to the inside of the cell. The neuraminidase glycoproteins function in what may appear to be the opposite manner. Neuraminidase is an enzyme that removes the molecules that the hemagglutinin binds to from the surface of the cell. Although this function may seem to be deleterious to the function of the hemagglutinin, the neuraminidase function is important in that it allows new viruses to float away from the cell after they have been assembled. Without the neuraminidase glycoprotein, the viruses would remain attached to the cell in which they were assembled.

Since we now know that avian influenza hemagglutinin and neuraminidase glycoproteins function in virus entry and release, we can explore the specificity that these molecules convey to the virus subtypes. All 15 hemagglutinin molecules can mediate entry for the virus into bird cells. However, the avian influenza virus is not restricted to bird species. Many of the hemagglutinin molecules can recognize receptors that are displayed on the cells of other species. The hemagglutinin subtypes H1, H2, H3, and H5 can mediate infection into human cells and the hemagglutinin subtypes H1 and H3 have been shown to infect pig cells. Furthermore, H3 and H7 can confer the ability to infect horse cells (Table 3.1). Since avian influenza viruses, especially strains such as H3, can result in entry to multiple hosts, the potential for deadly recombination is high. This type of infection in multiple hosts has often been the cause of pandemics. The neuraminidase glycoprotein also exhibits species specificity, as it is not effective in all species. However, it should be noted that these components of the virus are not the only determinants of host range. Most, if not all, of the internal components play some role in determining host range. The hemagglutinin and neuraminidase components do specify the entry events, but the capsid components also play a role in the replication cycle. Work in this field has demonstrated that entry into a cell does not necessarily result in replication and assembly of progeny virus.

### THERE'S A LOT IN A NAME

The nomenclature (naming system) of the avian influenza viruses is slightly more complicated than the simplified hemagglutinin and neuraminidase designation described above. The current nomenclature names the virus based on the host of origin of the virus, the geography of the first virus isolation, the number of isolates, the year that the virus was isolated, and the major type of hemagglutinin and

**Table 3.1** Hemagglutinin helps direct the avian influenza virus through the body. This chart shows the hemagglutinin subtypes that mediate infection in humans, pigs, horses, and birds.

| STRAIN | HOST RANGE | | | |
|---|---|---|---|---|
| H1 | Human | Pig | | Bird |
| H2 | Human | | | Bird |
| H3 | Human | Pig | Horse | Bird |
| H4 | | | | Bird |
| H5 | Human | | | Bird |
| H6 | | | | Bird |
| H7 | | | Horse | Bird |
| H8 | | | | Bird |
| H9 | | | | Bird |
| H10 | | | | Bird |
| H11 | | | | Bird |
| H12 | | | | Bird |
| H13 | | | | Bird |
| H14 | | | | Bird |
| H15 | | | | Bird |

neuraminidase glycoproteins. For example, Ty/Mass/3740/65 (H6N2) is an avian influenza virus that was isolated from a turkey in Massachusetts. The virus was isolate number 3,740 and was found in 1965. Of course, since the hemagglutinin

## DRUGS TO FIGHT INFLUENZA

Drugs designed to combat viral infections have been difficult to produce and use. The primary reason for this difficulty has been the nature of viral infection. This is especially true for influenza virus infections; viral infections are usually severe. The influenza virus attacks the lungs and rapidly causes disease. Shortly after the symptoms of the infection are being felt, the host's immune system starts to take control of the virus's replication. This creates a small window of opportunity in which a drug can be effective. Despite this challenge, drugs against the influenza virus were among the first antiviral agents ever devised. The drugs amantadine and rimantadine have been used for many years. Both drugs prevent the virus from gaining access to the host cell's nucleus and have been shown to also affect the assembly of the virus through effects on the hemagglutinin glycoprotein. The other major surface protein of the influenza virus, the neuraminidase glycoprotein, is the target of a new class of drugs, appropriately called neuraminidase inhibitors. The drugs zanamivir and oseltamivir were designed using a new technology called rational drug design that takes advantage of the structures of the target protein. The process is similar to a complicated three-dimensional puzzle that ensures the tightest fit possible for a small molecule into clefts on the neuraminidase glycoprotein. Both drugs are generally used as prophylactic (preventative) agents in high-risk populations during flu season.

and neuraminidase subtypes are specified (H6N2), the virus is implied to be a type A virus. The hemagglutinin and neuraminidase glycoproteins of type B and type C influenza viruses are not categorized into subtypes.

# 4

# Crossing Species: A Virus of Birds, Pigs, and Man

**All pathogenic viruses have developed an ecological niche. That is, viruses** usually find a host that will support their replication without routinely causing the host to succumb to the disease caused by the resulting infection. This relationship between a tolerating host and its virus makes up the reservoir of the virus, which is a persistent source of the virus to the surrounding ecology. Establishing this type of relationship between the host and the virus requires many decades. Although a precise mechanism has not been defined for establishing a reservoir, different forces may be involved. Selective pressure leads to an increase in the number of organisms that have characteristics or modifications beneficial to their survival and reproduction. Over time, these characteristics become an established feature of the organism. The process by which an organism gains these beneficial characteristics is called adapation. Adaptation is a critical component of evolution. The virus could eventually evolve to evade the host's immune system, to a point where it sufficiently mimics the host's own cellular components. This could be achieved by modification of the surface of the virus's components to look like those of the host, such as by the addition of an exterior shield designed to resemble the glycoproteins that cover the host's cells. Thus, the host's immune system can no longer distinguish the virus from the body's own cells and is no longer effective at removing the virus from the body. However, this mechanism is only half of the story since it only describes the way that tolerance by the host is generated. The other half of the story is that the virus itself becomes less virulent, or less able to cause disease. Experimental devices have demonstrated that a virus does actually adapt to the cells it infects so that continued replication is optimized. The selection of viruses that can maintain replication is probably achieved through a simple mechanism. If the virus becomes overly virulent, the long-term survival of the viruse is at risk. Eventually, the host succumbs to the disease brought on by the virus and the virulent pathogen cannot be passed on to another host. This type of mechanism suggests that overly aggressive viruses are self-limiting. That is, the virus destroys the host in which it is replicating, effectively eliminating all available resources. However, the less virulent strains of the virus can be selected and maintained throughout a local population by not causing disease in the host. The viruses that do not cause disease have two advantages. First, the virus can continue to replicate without destroying the host, thereby increasing its chances of being spread to other hosts. The second advantage is that the host itself does not appear to be a diseased member of the community. Nearly all species of animals have a natural tendency to exclude and avoid sick members of their community. This social defense mechanism has real implications in a pathogen's ecology. The hosts that are infected with a virus, but remain asymptomatic, are more likely to socialize with the community and thus are more likely to spread their disease. So, over many decades, selective pressures by the host on both a molecular and a social level generate a reservoir for a virus.

## WATERFOWL: THE RESERVOIR OF AVIAN FLU

Over 100 years of infections have generated a tolerance and persistence between wild waterfowl and avian influenza viruses. All of the makings of a reservoir have been generated over the century. The virus does not seem to cause disease in the wild waterfowl, yet persists in these birds as a continual source of virus to the environment. Most if not all of the influenza viruses infect avian species. In fact, birds provide an ideal species for persistent infections. From the standpoint of a virus, the most attractive characteristics of birds include their migratory nature and flocking characteristics. For example, before the fall migration, a family of geese (brood) begins assembling into small groups. The mating pairs of the group are lifetime partners, and their offspring are generally 4 to 6 weeks old by the fall season. Just after the beginning of the fall season, the individual broods begin gathering into one large group, or flock. On the North American continent, the flock gathers at lakes within the Canadian borders. These gathering places provide exceptional opportunities for transmission of avian influenza, since the extremely large number of birds creates crowded conditions. One unfortunate detail is that nearly all waterfowl, including ducks and various geese, can be infected with the avian flu.

The transmission of the flu virus between birds is some-what different than the mode of transmission between humans. Since the influenza virus replicates in the lungs of mammals, the medium for exchange of virus between humans is usually a cough or a sneeze from an infected individual. However, the virus may also spread when someone touches an object, such as a doorknob or table, that is contaminated with the virus and then touches his or her eyes or mouth. The simple act of a hand-to-face movement actually serves to inoculate one's own body with the virus. The transmission of the flu virus between birds occurs in a different manner. The virus replicates in the intestinal tract of infected birds and therefore is easily spread between birds by the exchange of bodily excretions. If you have ever been to a pond or lake that is occupied by migrating geese or even a family of ducks, you may have noticed that birds are not conscientious about sanitation. The birds' feces are often spread on the ground, sometimes even mixed throughout the bread or corn that people throw on the ground for the birds to eat. Thus, it is not difficult to comprehend that the most common mode of transmission of the flu virus between birds is through a fecal-to-oral transmission route. Thus, when a goose eats something that an infected bird has defecated onto, the goose ingests inoculants of the avian influenza virus. Furthermore, excrement from infected birds contaminates the surrounding waterways. This contaminated water can also act as a vehicle for inoculation. The birds drink, and bathe and swim in, this water. These acts provide the virus with access to the digestive tract. So, birds can spread the virus in many different ways. The flock's close community for sleeping and eating produces nearly optimal conditions for transmission of avian flu. Living in a close community is probably one of the causes of high incidence of infection among waterfowl.

These conditions are not limited to an isolated pond, but instead are spread along the migratory routes of the birds. The initial spreading of avian influenza between flocks may occur in the fall at a lake in Canada. As the geese fly south for the winter, they carry the virus with them. The virus then gets deposited at each small lake, pond, golf course, or any other resting spot along the way. However, the deposited virus is not simply left there. Local ponds in America contain ducks and other waterfowl that reside at the pond year-round. These fowl are susceptible to infection from the virus and also add to the spread of the virus. Thus, a new strain of avian influenza has the potential to spread over an entire continent in a single migratory season.

Asia has a more severe problem with avian influenza. The problem is not due to the migratory route taken by wild ducks and geese. Instead, the problem in Asia is primarily due to social habits among the continent's people. The people of Asia prefer fresh poultry. This preference for fresh foods is very common among the people of different countries. Each region of the world has an inclination for raising or growing different foods. These foods often become a way of life or a delicacy for the region's culture. The preference for the people of China is for a bird to be brought home alive before it is to be served at a dinner. Although this may seem odd to traditional American cultures, the habit would be as normal as bringing home a watermelon on the Fourth of July or a bag of lettuce from the local grocery store for evening dinner. In some Asian cultures, people may raise fowl at their homes for consumption. However, the majority of Asian citizens purchase these birds from local markets.

## TROUBLE AT THE MARKET

For China, food markets often provide the location for the primary transfer of avian influenza between wild and domestic avian species. These markets have catered to the demands of the Asian people and have evolved over centuries; the markets of China are absolutely the best place to find fresh ducks and geese. A person may walk into these markets and purchase a goose or a duck of any size or shape. Additionally, turkeys, chickens, pheasants, quail, and pigeons can be purchased and placed on a dinner table the same evening (Figure 4.1). Furthermore, other nonavian species can also be purchased here. Pigs, fish, lambs, and exotic species can be purchased live in these markets. Pigs will be discussed later; they represent the biggest threat of avian influenza for humans. Bear in mind that chicken, ducks, and geese do not necessarily have to be raised on farms to represent a threat to humans. In fact, the mixing of wild and domesticated birds results in efficient transfer of avian influenza viruses between the birds. The markets of Chinese cities provide the best environment for this type of transfer because of the high demand for fresh goods and rich diversity of a metropolitan city. Chinese people who live in the city, have the opportunity to purchase a vast selection of foods. These foods many include

**Figure 4.1** Unsanitary conditions where avian species congregate, such as food and poultry markets, contribute to the spread of the virus.

fresh chicken, ducks, and geese. However, not all of these animals are grown as domesticated poultry, and not all of the animals will be sold on the day that they are brought to the market. For the consumers, these facts increase the likelihood for the spread of avian influenza.

An Asian market often has cages of birds stacked upon one another. These birds share common water and food sources and their excrement is often splattered on the cages. When the market closes in the evening, a shopkeeper may decide to bring his unsold birds back home to his farm. If his unsold birds were exposed to the avian influenza virus, then the shopkeeper will unwittingly bring the avian influenza back home to all of his other birds. The minimum consequence for this act is that the virus infects his flocks, and his birds start producing fewer eggs and become thinner. Thus the shopkeeper's livelihood is immediately at risk. The shopkeeper may rely on the eggs and birds to feed his family. He may also rely on these birds for monetary income so that he may buy clothes and other foods. Now, the infected birds will not produce enough eggs to feed his family and no one will buy his thin birds. After all, no one dreams of a nice "thin" turkey, and most people desire the fattest and healthiest of birds for their meals. The shopkeeper may have no idea what happened to his birds, but the spread of the avian influenza virus from a wild bird to a domesticated bird, and then into the home, resulted in a great threat to his livelihood and possibly even his health. This type of devastation can wipe out an entire region. The markets are often filled with birds from many farmers. Each of these farmers may bring home the avian influenza virus and suffer the same fate of sick birds and low egg output. This unfortunate outcome then spreads to the rest of the community. The lower income for the farmers means that they can no longer buy goods from the other vendors at the market. These vendors suffer from lower incomes and the economic impact begins to snowball until the country begins to feel the impact of a weak economy. For poorer regions, this impact can devastate the entire infrastructure.

The impact on the local farmers and indirectly on the regional economy is a harsh and cruel result of the avian influenza virus. However, this indirect effect is often difficult to perceive. A farmer usually does not consider the impact his actions may have to the gross national product of his country. His only concern is likely how to bring home food to his family. Therefore, he may actually contribute to the spread of the virus when he brings his sick birds to the market. However, the avian flu is not limited to spread among bird species, and when mutations in the virus allow a leap to mammals, the local people become painfully aware of the impact the avian influenza can have.

As was discussed in Chapter 3, some of the strains of avian influenza can infect birds, pigs, humans, and horses. For example, viruses containing the H1 and H3 glycoprotein can infect birds, pigs, and humans. In fact, it was an avian influenza virus containing the H1 glycoprotein that caused the 1918 influenza pandemic, and a virus containing the H3 glycoprotein that caused the 1957 pandemic. Although these viruses are not considered to be avian influenza viruses, the viruses do contain many of the components of the avian strains. The relationship that has been drawn recently is actually another result of the food markets. A bird that is infected with the avian influenza virus may transmit the virus to a pig or to a human. The results of this infection can often be much more deadly in the pigs and humans than in the birds. Furthermore, the avian viruses may combine with other mammalian viruses to generate pathogens with the potential to cause pandemics that could cripple entire countries.

This potential of the avian influenza virus to generate deadly diseases in markets has been realized by the World Health Organization. This global organization has pressured governments to better regulate the local markets. The intention of these regulations is to improve the sanitation of the markets and to prevent the mixing of species that could allow multiple influenza viruses to combine and cause deadly pandemics. The city of Hong Kong has adopted many of the measures suggested by the World Health Organization and has been successful at eradicating avian influenza from its markets. The scare of a new avian influenza virus that was first detected in 1997 prompted the implementation of several regulations, which were sequentially passed by the local government. Since it was known that ducks and geese are the primary reservoir of the avian influenza virus, these species were banned from the markets in 1998. Two years later, the

**Figure 4.2** A market worker cleans the cages used at the Asian markets. This has proven to be an effective step to prevent the spread of the virus.

government imposed a requirement to close the market one day during every month. On this day, the markets are closed to commerce and sanitized. The improvement in sanitation was designed to prevent the persistent spread of the virus over several months. One year later, in 2001, quails were found at be susceptible to the new strain of avian influenza and were also banned from the markets. The subsequent regulations took a more active role at cleaning the markets of avian influenza. An active bird vaccination protocol was implemented on all farms that contributed birds to the market in 2002. Furthermore, an additional cleaning day was implemented, making the market closed two days during every month for the purpose of sanitation (Figure 4.2). The most

## THE CONFORMATIONAL CHANGE OF THE INFLUENZA VIRUS HEMAGGLUTININ GLYCOPROTEIN

Much of the knowledge of virus entry, as mediated by the viral glycoprotein, is founded on experiments performed with the hemagglutinin molecule of the influenza virus. The influenza virus hemagglutinin is packed on the outside of influenza virions and appears as spikes on the surface of the virus. These molecules reach out and bind specific molecules on the surface of the target cell that the virus is going to infect. In particular, the virus binds to sialic acid molecules that are abundant on the surface of most cells. The portion of the molecule that binds to the sialic acid is at the very top of the hemagglutinin molecule. After binding, the influenza virus hemagglutinin responds to specific signals from the cells to trigger a conformational change in the molecule. The conformational change causes a portion of the hemagglutinin glycoprotein, known as the fusion peptide, to insert into the target membrane. Conformational recent measure was imposed in 2003 and strengthened the vaccination requirements of local farms for avian influenza and required an inspection of all birds to be sold. The inspection procedure became known as biosecurity. All of these regulations were deemed successful in entirely removing avian influenza from the city. In 2004, the new strain of avian influenza could not be found anywhere in Hong Kong. However, Shenzhen, a city that is just 35 kilometers away from Hong Kong, did not implement these rules in their markets and continues to have problems with avian influenza. This convincing story of the successful eradication of a virus from a market proves that local measures by a government can produce worldwide effects.

change that the proteins undergo in response to signals from the cell was an extraordinary discovery made by two scientists, Don Wiley and Sir John Skehel. Dr. Wiley was a scientist at Harvard University in Boston, Massachusetts and was a colleague and a competitor of Dr. Skehel, who was at the National Institute for Medical Research in London, England. Fortunately, the two gentlemen chose, in the spirit of scientific discovery, to collaborate in the design of pioneering experiments in the discovery of molecular structures. Wiley's and Skehel's discovery showed virologists how viral proteins could mediate membrane fusion and showed structural biologists that proteins could undergo massive conformational changes. Today, the conformational change that the influenza virus hemagglutinin glycoprotein undergoes is known as a "spring-loaded" mechanism and is the basis of the world's current understanding of virus entry.

# 5

# The H5N1 Avian Flu

In 1997, the newest strain of avian influenza to emerge out of Asia caught the attention of the entire world. The virus is still mostly limited to avian species, but has been identified in the deaths of at least 20 people. Fear of the virus is having enormous social and economic impact throughout the world.

## WHERE DID H5N1 COME FROM?

As mentioned in the previous chapter, when avian influenza viruses infect different species, they create the potential for switching the avian components of the virus with the components of different influenza strains that have already adapted to infect that species. The process that creates a new virus through reassortment of different components is known as **antigenic shift**. This shift in the composition of the virus occurs dramatically and often results in a virus with a different host range and different degrees of the disease caused by the virus. The influenza viruses possess eight different components and the genetic makeup of these viruses allows the components to be easily exchanged when different viruses infect the same cell. As mentioned previously, the 1957 Asian flu contained the H2N2 glycoproteins. This virus caused the deaths of more than one million people worldwide. The source of this virus was quite possibly the unregulated Asian poultry markets that were described in the previous chapter. The eight components of the H2N2 virus were clearly obtained from reassortment of influenza viruses that had adapted to different species. Three of the components were derived from the circulating avian influenza found in ducks that year, and the remaining five components were derived from the circulating human pool. The resulting H2N2 virus possessed the ability to evade detection by the human immune system, and possessed the disease-causing capabilities of the avian influenza. The H2N2 virus also retained the ability to replicate in humans and was transmitted from human to human. The characteristics of the virus created a catastrophic combination. However, one of the most interesting features of this new virus is that the actual reassortment of the virus's components seemed to have taken place in a pig. The evidence that a cross-species reassortment had taken place was that some of the genes of the H2N2 virus had components that were previously restricted to pigs, yet also retained some components of the avian virus. Although the genetic and biochemical evidence for this occurrence is very strong, the events that would be required for this reassortment to occur are difficult to imagine. Yet, the Asian markets provide the ideal setting for a human and a bird, which are both infected with a type A influenza virus, to be in the same vicinity as a pig. In this case, the pig is believed to have been infected with both viruses. The viruses that were being shed by the pig then infected other humans, and quite possibly other birds. The new virus could also be transmitted between humans. The ravages of the virus are now documented.

The events that cause an antigenic shift are easily conceived when the potential for reassortment is provided. However, a reassortment is not always required. The most devastating influenza pandemic was caused in 1918 by the H1N1 influenza strain, which killed 50 million people worldwide. This virus did not appear to undergo reassortment, but instead was able to acquire the ability to cross species through mutations in the bird, a trait that is alarming to scientists who study influenza viruses. However, the evidence of antigenic drift in the H1N1 virus cannot rule out a progressive transfer of the virus between species prior to reaching humans. Since the H1N1 virus is known to infect pigs as well as humans, the Asian markets may have again provided the setting for the transmission of the deadly virus to humans by creating a situation where all three species are in close proximity to one another. It is not only possible, but likely that the H1N1 virus was first transmitted from a bird to a pig and then to a human. Once all eight of the virus components had acquired the ability to replicate and be transmitted by humans, the virus rapidly spread around the world.

The newest strain of the avian influenza virus that is circulating in wild waterfowl is the H5N1 avian influenza virus. This virus infects a wide variety of avian species, including the usual host species—ducks, geese, and chickens—but is not limited to these birds. Birds with vast migratory ranges (such as the black headed gulls, feral pigeons, little egrets, grey herons, and peregrine falcons) and migratory shore-birds in Russia and Siberia have also been infected and can spread the virus across continents. The full name of the H5N1 avian influenza virus is more revealing of the virus that was initially isolated by scientists. The circulating H5N1 virus that is the current source of fear throughout the world is officially named A/Goose/Guangdong/1/96 (H5N1). This name clearly indicates that the one strain of the type A influenza virus subtype H5N1 was isolated in 1996 from a goose that lived in the Guangdong province of China. When the strain was identified by normal surveillance of the circulating virus, it was alarming since this was the first time that the virus had been identified as a prevalent circulating avian influenza virus in China. Just a few months after the virus was discovered, the greatest fears of those surveying the spread of influenza were realized. The H5N1 virus was transmitted from a bird to a human. In May of 1997, a 3-year-old child from China became infected with the virus and developed a severe respiratory illness. Unfortunately, the child became the first human casualty of the H5N1 virus. Fears continued to escalate during the next flu season.

During the fall flu season in 1997, the virus continued to spread and reassortment began diversifying the circulating strains. Geese continued to be the primary host of the H5N1 virus, but evidence that the virus had reassorted with the circulating avian influenza viruses of a quail H9N2 and a duck H6N1 had emerged. Transmission to the human population was also becoming apparent. During November and December of 1997, a total of 18 human cases of H5N1 virus infection were confirmed. Of these 18 cases, an alarmingly high proportion resulted in death. One-third of those infected died from the disease caused by the virus. Transmission from birds to humans now seemed to be a real capability of the virus. Additionally, the virus that was transmitted appeared to contain many of the characteristics of the avian H5N1 virus and exhibited little evidence of reassortment to infect humans. The deadly H5N1 virus appears to possess all eight components in high similarity to the avian species, and these characteristics are retained when the virus is transmitted to humans. Thus, the virus appeared to have acquired the ability to infect humans through antigenic drift, in a manner similar to the H1N1 virus.

The deadly characteristics of this virus in humans lead to the categorization of the virus into the "highly pathogenic" category of influenza viruses. The term **pathogenic** refers to the severity of disease caused by the virus. Although it may seem obvious that a highly pathogenic influenza virus causes severe disease and a low pathogenic virus causes a more mild or undetectable disease, the components of the virus that dictate this characteristic are less clear. The hemagglutinin glycoprotein clearly correlates with the virus's pathogenicity, but the host and the remaining seven components also play a role. From 1997 through 2002, the H5N1 virus continued its antigenic drift and also its increase in geographic prevalence. Detection of the virus was mostly restricted to the

**Figure 5.1** Dead birds, especially domesticated chickens that have been raised on farms, are indicators of avian flu.

geese of southern China. The virus did not appear to exhibit high pathogenicity in these birds. However, in domesticated chickens that were raised on farms, the virus was highly pathogenic (Figure 5.1). Ducks, like geese, also seemed to be more tolerant of the infections. Exceptions to this rule sporadically emerged. In 2002, the virus was isolated from wild migrating birds and had apparently become highly pathogenic. One such example was in a public park in Hong Kong.

In December 2002, numerous aquatic birds were found dead in the Kowloon Park. The H5N1 virus was isolated from these birds and determined to be the cause of their death. This was the first appearance of a highly pathogenic virus in wild aquatic birds and indicated that the trend of the virus's evolution was toward a more pathogenic virus instead of a less pathogenic virus (Figure 5.2).

The virus also continued to infect humans and reports of direct transmission between birds and humans could be found. Among the reports were also indications that the virus could potentially be transmitted from human to human. In February 2003, a Chinese family visited the Fujian province of southeastern China. The family planned to visit relatives and celebrate the lunar New Year. This celebration is often a week-long festival for the people of China and is always accompanied with delicious foods. However, the prevalence of the avian flu and the high demand for fresh poultry turned the celebration into a nightmare for one family. The family had two children, a daughter and a son.

During the New Year celebration in Fujan, China, the daughter was in close contact with living birds and became infected with avian influenza. She died within days of becoming ill. The rapid onset of the disease prevented the family from returning home to seek care for the girl, so their daughter died in the town where she was infected with the virus. Immediately after her death, the family returned home to Hong Kong, China. Upon arriving home, both the father and his son developed symptoms of influenza. The father died soon after returning home, but his son was able to recover. This report was alarming for several reasons. First, it was evidence of the severe nature of the circulating virus. The virus could not only kill avian species, but it also could rapidly kill humans. In this case, two out of three people infected died from the disease. The third person in

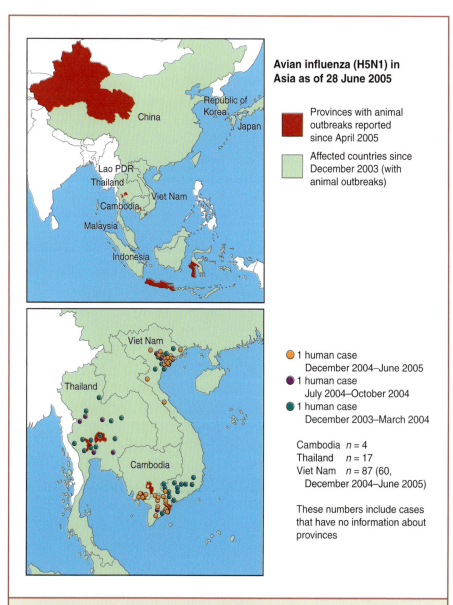

**Avian influenza (H5N1) in Asia as of 28 June 2005**

■ Provinces with animal outbreaks reported since April 2005

■ Affected countries since December 2003 (with animal outbreaks)

● 1 human case December 2004–June 2005
● 1 human case July 2004–October 2004
● 1 human case December 2003–March 2004

Cambodia  $n = 4$
Thailand    $n = 17$
Viet Nam   $n = 87$ (60, December 2004–June 2005)

These numbers include cases that have no information about provinces

**Figure 5.2**  The H5N1 avian influenza virus was discovered in Asia in the late 1990s. By 2002, the virus had become highly pathogenic in wild aquatic birds. The H5N1 strain has exhibited a trend of pathogenic evolution that makes it a serious threat to human health.

this case was so ill that he was hospitalized and unable to care for himself. This report also indicated that the virus may have started to gain the third characteristic of the three traits defined by the World Health Organization required to cause a deadly pandemic: evidence of human-to-human transmission was emerging. The fact that the father and son showed indications of infection with the avian influenza virus after the daughter had already succumbed to the disease suggested that the actual infection was a separate occurrence. The family could clearly describe the likely source of the infection for the daughter, but could not describe the source of the infection for the father and son. Thus, a strong possibility for a case of human-to-human transmission had been presented.

The trend toward a more pathogenic virus continued in 2003, and it became apparent that the virus was becoming a real threat to human health in 2004. A new strain was isolated in Vietnam and named A/Vietnam/1203/04 (H5N1). This virus exhibited highly pathogenic characteristics. No longer could birds tolerate the disease. In fact, domesticated birds on farms did not even seem to have a chance to combat the virus before they died. Chickens that became infected with the virus died within 24 hours. Wild aquatic birds such as ducks fared slightly better than their domesticated cousins. Wild ducks that became infected with the newly defined H5N1 virus generally died within 48 hours.

The virus has also continued to infect humans. During the 14 months that followed December 2003, there were a confirmed 97 cases of human infections by the avian influenza H5N1 virus. Consistent with the highly pathogenic nature of the virus, 53 of the 97 people died as a result of the infection. Most of these people had contact with birds, suggesting that the transmission was the result of direct bird-to-human transfer. However, the potential of an intermediate host (like the pig in the 1957 outbreak) exists for the current strain as well. Pigs are susceptible to the avian influenza virus and the virus does replicate in pigs. Yet, the virus has not developed the capacity for pig-to-pig transmission; this is similar to the virus's restricted transmission in humans. However, concern of a potential intermediate host does exist. Cats have been identified as hosts for the H5N1 avian influenza and the virus has developed the ability to spread between cats through direct transmission. Although there is concern for potential reassortment, the probability of this occurring is still quite low. After all, how often are birds and

## OTHER AVIAN INFLUENZA STRAINS THAT POSE SIGNIFICANT RISKS

Only influenza type A viruses infect birds and many of these viruses can also infect humans. Among the different hemagglutinin glycoproteins that are prevalent in birds, H5 and H7 seem to pose the primary threat. Both of these subtypes have been documented in a highly pathogenic form and each can combine with all nine of the neuraminidase glycoproteins. A third hemagglutinin glycoprotein, H9, can also be combined with each of the neuraminidases, but H9 has only been documented in the low pathogenic form.

These avian viruses can also be transmitted to the human population. For instance, the H9N2 virus caused mild illness in several people from 1998 to 2003. All of these cases were restricted to China and Hong Kong. Additionally, the highly pathogenic H7 strain has also been transmitted to humans and seems to be present in countries outside of Asia. The H7 hemagglutinin has been combined with N2 and N3 in North America and with N7 in the Netherlands. The H7N3 virus was found in a sick person in Canada that had an eye infection. Luckily, the infection was mild and the person was able to return cats kept close to one another? Whether the H5N1 virus uses an intermediate host or not, the potential for reassortment that produces a pandemic still exists. The possibility remains that the H5N1 virus could infect a human that is already infected with the circulating human influenza. The infection of a single person by both of these viruses provides the opportunity for the virus to gain the characteristic of human-to-human transmission. It is the lack of this route of transmission that currently precludes the pandemic potential of the H5N1 virus.

home shortly after being hospitalized. The person was apparently infected at work, a poultry farm. The H7N2 virus was detected in a man that was admitted to the emergency room in New York in 2003. The person was extremely ill and exhibited respiratory distress. After several weeks in the hospital, the person recovered and was sent home. Unfortunately, a source of the virus was never determined. This person did not work with birds, and could not remember being in direct contact with birds before he was infected. The H7N7 strain occurred in an outbreak on several farms in the Netherlands. This strain was particularly alarming because it infected a total of 89 humans and several pigs during the outbreak. Although most of those infected exhibited only mild symptoms, approximately 10 exhibited more severe flu-like symptoms. A veterinarian that visited one of the infected farms died from an infection of H7N7. These other viruses have demonstrated the potential for severe symptoms due to infections in humans, but have not exhibited the capacity for human-to-human transmission.

# 6

# Is Another Pandemic Lurking Among the Flock?

The trend exhibited by the H5N1 strain has alerted officials around the world to prepare for another possible deadly influenza pandemic. From worldwide organizations to local governments, plans are being implemented to lessen the destruction that could be created by this virus. The primary measures include containing the spread of the virus and preparing vaccines for the strain of the virus that may ultimately reach the human population.

## PREVENTING THE SPREAD OF AVIAN INFLUENZA IN ASIA

The most logical and primary concern of WHO is to stop the spread of the H5N1 strain. However, this has proven to be an extraordinarily difficult task. The virus is currently spread from region to region and from country to country by migratory birds. An organization cannot stop this seasonal migration any more than ducks and geese can be prevented from socializing around the lakes and ponds before they prepare for migration. However, government organizations do have the ability to regulate the people that control domesticated birds on farms and in the markets. Birds that are more susceptible to infection by avian flu have been banned from being sold in Asian markets. The measure to prevent certain bird species from intermixing within the market proved to be successful in creating a modest improvement in containing the avian influenza virus within certain species. The markets were also asked to close down for 2 days every month. On the days that the markets were closed, the employees in the markets thoroughly cleaned the entire market. The bird cages were disinfected and the floors and walls were scrubbed. Since the mechanism of transmission for the virus is via a fecal-to-oral route, the cleaning days were intended to remove the fecal material that is the primary source of avian influenza viruses. The material was cleaned from the bowls and the cages as well. The seemingly modest regulations were successfully implemented in Hong Kong. The Hong Kong markets became free of avian influenza viruses shortly after implementing the disinfection regulations. Apparently, the act of cleaning the cages was beneficial for the prevention of spread within the market. The effectiveness of the regulations was underscored by the discovery that Hong Kong's markets were entirely clean and free of avian influenza viruses, including the prevalent H5N1 strain. However, a neighboring city was still suffering from the effects of the virus.

Although the cleaning days for the markets did help stop the spread of the virus, it did not prevent new virus from coming into the markets. Stronger measures had to be implemented to prevent farmers from bringing in birds that were infected with avian influenza. The most logical method of preventing infected birds from entering the market would be to ask the farmers to immediately report evidence of a new infection. Additionally, the farmers would be asked to not bring these birds or any other birds from their farm into the markets. This was attempted, but was not successful. More birds that were obviously infected with avian influenza were still coming into the market. The government agencies realized that the voluntary efforts of the farmers would not be an effective method for control. The farmers relied on the income they earned from the market. Furthermore, the farmers often owned hundreds of ducks and geese. If a single duck was found dead with symptoms that were similar to the symptoms of avian influenza, the farmer would naturally try to hide the death. If the farmer announced the death, he would have to destroy his entire flock. The entire farm would be destroyed and the farmer may be faced with the prospect of being without income for several months to several years. A similar analogy could be drawn to the early farmers of North America. What if these farmers had been asked to destroy their entire crop if they found a pathogen on one of their fruit trees? They would be without income for 2 to 3 years since they would have destroyed the crop that they used to produce the income. As a result, the farmers may at the very least lose their homes. However, this would be a blessing compared to the losses that potentially could occur. In fact, North American farmers did suffer severe consequences for losing their sources of incomes during colonial times. If a farmer could not afford medicine for a sick child, then the child might die. This sentence was not limited to the children of the family, but could also occur to the father or the mother. If one of the parents of a family died during the early settlement of North America, then the entire family would face enormous hurdles for their own survival. The prospect of excelling in society or achieving the American dream that they had initially sought could evaporate. If the Asian poultry farmer was to follow the regulations of the government and report the potential infection of his flock, similar, potentially severe consequences could face him.

Although the government did require that the poultry farmers report outbreaks of avian flu, some degree of non-compliance is expected. Therefore, the Asian governments also imposed mandatory inspections on the poultry farmers. When a single farm is identified with an outbreak of avian influenza, the entire farm is quarantined. Every bird on the farm is **culled**, or killed (Figure 6.1). The farm is then disinfected. Culling and disinfection are two of the most drastic and costly of prevention methods, but are also the most effective. The culling process can also be scaled up to secure entire regions infected with avian influenza. Hong Kong, which has

**Figure 6.1** Health workers prepare to cull ducks on an infected farm. Culling and disinfection are effective methods of eliminating avian flu from farms.

been the most successful at containing the H5N1 virus, controlled the outbreaks by culling approximately 1.5 million birds in 1997 alone, in addition to imposing the strictest poultry market regulations. Once the birds are culled, the carcasses are disposed of in a manner that prevents further spread of the disease. This usually involves burning the carcasses in a mass grave. Since 1997, hundreds of millions of birds have been culled.

## THE INEFFECTIVENESS OF EFFECTIVE VACCINES

Every fall, most cities in the United States provide their citizens with an opportunity to receive a vaccine against the circulating strain of the influenza virus. The vaccine has been demonstrated to be effective in generating immunity to the disease caused by influenza viruses.

Vaccines are generally used to prime a body's immune system for an encounter with a pathogen. A properly designed vaccine would ideally recognize a pathogen as soon as it entered the body. For example, a person who is vaccinated against the influenza virus may come into contact with the virus during the flu season. When the virus enters the body, the vaccine has prepared the immune system to quickly respond to the virus. Therefore, the response can be rapid and specific. The immune system may stop the virus from infecting a single cell, but more likely, the virus is halted after a few replication cycles have been completed. In the majority of cases, the vaccinated body is able to prevent a disease from manifesting.

The process of vaccination involves exposing the body to an inactivated or isolated component of a pathogen. In the case of influenza vaccines, both approaches are used. A live virus may be grown in chicken eggs. The live virus is isolated from the egg and then inactivated by treating the solution with formalin or beta-propriolactone, two chemicals routinely used in sterilization techniques. These types of production processes use whole inactivated virus for the vaccine. Alternatively, the purified virus can be further fractionated (divided) through a process that also inactivates the virus, but does not chemically modify the components of the virus. The latter method, known as subviral virus vaccination, usually involves using detergents that cause the virus to fall apart. After the virus is dissolved into pieces, the components that are normally on the surface of the intact virus are purified from the solution. The hemagglutinin and neuraminidase glycoproteins are the main targets of the immune system and are therefore the primary components that are targeted in vaccine design and production. Both the whole virus vaccine and the subviral vaccines are normalized based on the content or proportion of hemagglutinin molecules present in the preparation. Thus, a dose of the vaccine is based on the mass of the hemagglutinin proteins.

Fortunately, the hemagglutinin and neuraminidase glycoproteins elicit a strong immune response. Both are highly **immunogenic**. This characteristic of the glycoproteins makes them very effective at conferring immunity to the vaccinated person. However, as was described above, the glycoproteins are also capable of rapid mutation, which is the basis of immune evasion. Therefore, two questions are presented to vaccine design: With all of the available subtypes of viruses, which virus glycoprotein will be used for the current season's vaccine, and will the virus mutate before the vaccine is produced? The first question is answered every year by the Centers for Disease Control and Provention (CDC) and the influenza vaccine manufacturers in the United States. The CDC monitors the spread of the influenza virus every year. Surprisingly, the virus follows a very routine path, starting in China, then traveling to Russia. From Russia, the virus travels to the southern hemisphere and then makes its way north to the United States. This around-the-world pathway allows samples of the virus to be obtained and studied every year prior to the virus's actual arrival into the United States. The CDC uses this data to understand which subtype is most likely to strike the United States and asks the vaccine manufacturers to design vaccines based on their recommendation. This method of design has been extremely effective in accurately predicting the strain of influenza virus that will eventually circulate in the United States. Only a couple of mistakes have been made in this process. One example of a recent mistake was in 2003 when the CDC predicted that a

South American isolate of the influenza virus would reach the United States. Instead, a strain that was originally isolated from China prevailed and the vaccine developed that year was largely ineffective at conferring immunity to the circulating strain. The second question is also answered through persistent monitoring of the virus as it spreads. The answers frequently require that modifications are made to the current production processes. Sometimes, the hemagglutinin or neuraminidase glycoproteins used in the vaccine require modification to keep pace with the genetic drift of the circulating strain.

So, the process seems simple. The CDC gives the manufacturers the correct strain of virus to produce a vaccine against. Then the manufacturers inject eggs with the correct virus. The final step is to isolate the virus, inactivate it, and then bottle it up for public use. However, significant hurdles exist within the manufacturing model (Figure 6.2). First, the process is susceptible to error. The eggs used in the process frequently become contaminated with bacteria. This causes the entire lot to be lost. Second, only about three doses of a vaccine are produced from each egg that does not become contaminated. Currently, about 300 million doses are created every year. This staggering number requires that at least 100 million eggs be inoculated with the virus every year to generate the vaccine. Thus, on the manufacturing side, hurdles exist that could turn a year's work into a worthless, unprofitable disaster. Unfortunately, these are not the only hurdles that exist. An additional hurdle that must be met is the business model of any stable company. After the vaccines have been generated in significant numbers, they must also be sold. Selling a vaccine in an environment that does not possess the threat of a highly pathogenic strain is difficult. For example, when this book was written, most Americans had not directly experienced an influenza pandemic. This lack of experience makes it difficult to understand the importance of protecting against influenza virus on a yearly basis.

# Vaccine Production, a Fragile System

Flu vaccines are biological products, not chemicals that can be cranked out in times of need, and are made fresh every year.

### January to May

**Virus selection**
▶ FDA advisory panel selects three strains
▶ CDC provides new strains of the seed virus to the FDA
▶ FDA distributes the three seed viruses to manufacturers

**Production begins**
▶ Seed virus is injected into fertilized chicken eggs; virus multiplies in incubated eggs

▶ Egg white is removed, virus is harvested
▶ Chemical treatment applied to inactivate virus

### June/July

**FDA tests to confirm production**
▶ Determines amount/yield of virus strains, purity and potency

▶ The three strains are blended into one vaccine by the manufacturer
▶ FDA licenses the vaccine

### August

**Filling/packaging**
▶ Virus is filled into vials and syringes
▶ Virus is packaged for distribution; kept in cold storage to ensure potency

### September

**Shipping**
Shipping of flu vaccine begins

### October/November

**Vaccination begins**
Immunity develops approximately 2 weeks after vaccination

SOURCE: Food and Drug Administration                                    AP

**Figure 6.2** Not all eggs used to create vaccines are successful. Frequently, eggs become contaminated and are thrown away. The process of vaccine production using eggs is illustrated here.

Furthermore, the current outbreaks of the highly pathogenic virus are restricted to Asian countries and do not show immediate signs of migration to America. Therefore, not all Americans see the need to purchase the influenza vaccine.

## A SHOT IN THE ARM FOR THE FLU VACCINE

The influenza vaccine during the 2004 flu season was in short supply. It seemed that panic over news of a potential pandemic was escalating and was being exacerbated by announcements that flu vaccine would not be available to most Americans. The looming shortage of the influenza vaccines became such a hot topic that President George W. Bush and then-presidential candidate John Kerry made the causes of the shortage a campaign issue. John Kerry accused the administration of failing to protect the American people from the influenza virus. Perhaps the basis of the accusation was centered on the perceived causes of the vaccine shortages during previous years. The Food and Drug Administration (FDA) imposed strict regulations on vaccine development known as Current Good Manufacturing Practices (CGMPs) that required noncompliant companies to invest millions of dollars into existing manufacturing plants. The requirements of the CGMPs forced two of the four American influenza vaccine manufacturers out of business, leaving Americans with only half the number of facilities to produce vaccines. Making matters worse, the remaining plants were making less money because of the additional money they were required to spend to upgrade their facilities to meet the new FDA regulations. Furthermore, all of the manufacturers are in constant threat of exorbitant awards to plaintiffs in lawsuits against the companies.

Fortunately for the vaccine manufacturers, the threat of the H5N1 strain will likely increase demand for their product in the coming years. However, the CDC predicts that during a deadly pandemic we will require on the order of billions of

This threat requires that the companies spend a large portion of the vaccine's manufacturing cost on liability insurance. If one influenza vaccine shot costs $5 in supplies, another $5 would have to be added for possible liability costs. These conditions imposed on vaccine manufacturers had weakened the incentives to generate the product. John Kerry argued that the government should re-evaluate the restrictions. The situation worsened in 2004 when a manufacturing plant contaminated their vaccine production. The fact that this contamination occurred in an election year charged the debate for vaccine-manufacturing reform.

George W. Bush won a second term as President during the 2004 election and has now met the need for reform with a new initiative of influenza-vaccine policy for the American people. President Bush's plan is to use $7.1 billion dollars to stockpile vaccines and drugs, and to continue to encourage manufacturers to upgrade their facilities. The money will directly help the manufacturers by creating a guarantee that their vaccine will be purchased after it has been generated. The hopes are that the money will also meet the needs required to protect Americans in the event that the avian flu becomes capable of being transmitted from person-to-person. A new government Website (http://pandemicflu.gov) has also been created to convey information about the potential pandemic.

doses of vaccine. Should the vaccine manufacturers begin staying ahead of the demand? The correct answer to these questions will require the government to guarantee that a certain percentage of the vaccines will be purchased. (Similar measures for assurance of income have been in place in the farming industry for years.)

The pending threat of the H5N1 avian flu strain has driven change in the vaccine industry (Figure 6.3). People are starting to become more aware of the need for effective vaccines. The recent high-profile reports of significant shortages of vaccine have been a strong impetus for governmental involvement. Furthermore, the manufacturers are developing more cost-effective tools for production. One promising tool is called "reverse genetics," which allows the manufacturers to steer away from eggs as vessels for production and turn instead to **tissue cultures**. Tissue culture would provide an easier system to manage with regards to contamination, would be more cost-effective, and would be easier to manipulate in order to keep up with the genetic drift of the influenza virus. Tissue culture systems require a large investment of capital to be implemented. The systems may require new factories to be built. The tissue culture facilities will have to be designed so that mammalian kidney cells, which are hardy cells that grow well in culture, can be produced on very large scale. The cultured cells will be infected with the FDA-designated influenza viruses for the given year. The virus will then continue to replicate in these cells, a process that can be continued indefinitely to generate large amounts of virus for vaccine use. The fact that the virus to be used for vaccine development is generated in mammalian cells also provides an advantage for use as an antigen. As the virus assembles and replicates in a cell, the cell modifies the virus. The modification by mammalian cells is slightly different than the modification generated by avian cells. The main differences are in the carbohydrate groups that are attached to the outside of the virus shell. Current use of

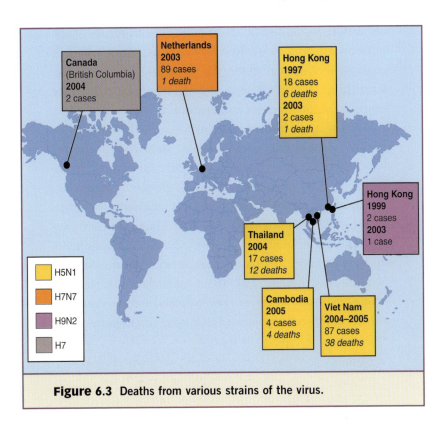

**Figure 6.3** Deaths from various strains of the virus.

chicken eggs generates viruses that have chicken carbohydrate groups. This seemingly subtle difference means that the virus may be rapidly detected when it initially enters a human, but once the virus begins to replicate it will acquire different carbohydrate groups and may not be recognized as well by the immune system. Thus the tissue culture system should generate a more effective vaccine, and do so at a lower cost to the manufacturer.

The avian influenza virus is a pathogen that continually circulates among wild and domesticated birds. However, the virus can occasionally mutate, becoming highly pathogenic and gaining the ability to infect and cause disease in humans. When the avian influenza virus made the leap from birds to humans, the results were devastating to the entire world population. In 1918, millions of people died because of the mutated influenza virus. In 1997, an avian influenza virus appeared in Asia that shows the potential to cause similar destruction. The H5N1 strain of avian influenza had already gained the ability to infect humans and has demonstrated the characteristics of a highly pathogenic virus. By the end of 2005, the H5N1 strain had caused serious illness in 124 people worldwide; 68 of those people died. If the virus mutates further and gains the capacity for person-to-person transmission, many more people will surely succumb to the virus. The threat posed by the H5N1 avian influenza virus has stimulated strong collaboration throughout the world. These collaborations toward a solution to an avian disease will improve the way scientists and the public think about human health. Ultimately, no one can be sure whether or not the H5N1 strain will emerge with the deadly consequences of its predecessors, but the world is watching and hopes to be ready.

# Glossary

**Antibody**—a Y-shaped molecule in the body that is secreted in response to a pathogen; antibodies are critical to adaptive immunity.

**Antigenic drift**—the continuous process of change over time in the influenza virus. The changes are usually the result of selective pressure by the host's immune system.

**Antigenic shift**—a sudden and abrupt change of antigenic variation among the influenza viruses. These changes are usually associated with the lack of a viable immune response and can be caused by genetic reassortment of different viruses.

***Bacillus anthracis***—a rod-shaped bacteria that causes the disease known as anthrax.

**Bacterium**—a unicellular prokaryotic organism that is capable of causing diseases in plants and animals.

**Capsid**—the inner shell of a virus that usually binds to and protects the nucleic acids. The capsid give the virus its characteristic shape.

**Culling**—the process of eliminating a disease by destroying farm animals that are infected with a pathogen.

**Electron microscope**—a high-powered microscope that magnifies an image using a steam of electrons.

**Epitope**—an influencing or determining element that mediates the interactions between an antibody and its target.

**Fermentable**—a substance that is capable of allowing organisms to anaerobically convert sugar to carbon dioxide and alcohol.

**Glycoprotein**—a polymeric amino acid chain that is conjugated to carbohydrate moieties.

**Hemagglutinin**—one of the surface components of the influenza virus. The molecule gets its name from its ability to cause the agglutination of red blood cells.

**Immune system**—the cells and molecules of the body that are designed to recognize and combat a disease.

**Immunity**—the state of being resistant to infection by a pathogen.

**Immunogenic**—capable of producing a response by the immune system.

**Influenza virus**—an RNA virus that causes respiratory illness in humans.

**Koch's postulates**—three requirements that must be experimentally demonstrated to define a pathogen as the cause of a disease.

# Glossary

**Microorganism**—an organism of microscopic or submicroscopic size.

**Mutagenesis**—the process of creating or generating changes in the genetic code of a gene.

**Neuraminidase**—an enzyme that removes sialic acid from the surface of molecules that usually line the gut and lungs.

**Obligatory pathogens**—microorganisms that cannot replicate outside the body of a host.

**Pandemic**—a wide distribution of an infectious disease over a large geographic range.

**Pasteurization**—the act of heating a solution for a specific amount of time for the purpose of destroying the microorganisms that may exist within it.

**Pathogen**—an infectious agent that causes a disease.

**Pathogenic**—able to cause disease.

**Progeny**—offspring or descendants.

**Quarantine**—a period of time that an object or organism is held under enforced isolation with the intentions of preventing the spread of a pathogen.

**Selective pressure**—a force or condition that can be naturally or artificially introduced to confer a growth advantage for one specimen over another.

**Spontaneous generation**—a disproven theory that microorganisms can be generated from thin air without parent organisms.

**Tissue culture**—a process of growing living tissue or cells in a Petri dish.

**Vaccine**—a disabled or fractionated component of a disease-causing organism that is injected into an organism to stimulate an immune response to that organism.

**Virion**—a complete viral particle consisting of the proteinaceous shell and genetic material of the virus.

# Notes

1. Abbott, A. Human fatality adds fresh impetus to fight against bird flu. *Nature* 423(6935) (2003): 5.

2. Aldhous, P. and S. Tomlin. Avian flu special: Avian flu: Are we ready? *Nature* 435(7041) (2005): 399.

3. Andresen, M. Avian flu: WHO prepares for the worst. *Canadian Medical Association Journal* 170(5) (2004): 777.

4. Baigent, S.J. and J.W. McCauley. Influenza type A in humans, mammals and birds: determinants of virus virulence, host-range and interspecies transmission. *Bioessays* 25(7) (2003): 657–71.

5. Bonn, D. Spared an influenza pandemic for another year? *Lancet* 349(9044) (1997): 36.

6. Brown, H. WHO confirms human-to-human avian flu transmission. *Lancet* 363(9407) (2004): 462.

7. Butler, D. Avian flu special: The flu pandemic: were we ready? *Nature* 435(7041) (2005): 400–402.

8. Centers for Disease Control and Prevention. Prevention and control of influenza: Recommendations of the Advisory Committee on Immunization Practices (ACIP). *MMWR Recommendations and Reports* 48(RR-4) (1999): 1–28.

9. Check, E. Avian flu special: Is this our best shot? *Nature* 435(7041) (2005): 404–6.

10. Chen, H., et al. The evolution of H5N1 influenza viruses in ducks in southern China. *Proceedings of the National Academy of Sciences USA* 101(28) (2004): 10452–7.

11. Cyranoski, D. Outbreak of chicken flu rattles Hong Kong. *Nature* 412(6844) (2001): 261.

12. Enserink, M. Infectious diseases. Avian flu outbreak sets off alarm bells. *Science* 300(5620) (2003): 718.

13. Enserink, M. and J. Kaiser. Virology. Avian flu finds new mammal hosts. *Science* 305(5689) (2004): 1385.

14. Enserink, M. and D. Normile. Infectious diseases. True numbers remain elusive in bird flu outbreak. *Science* 307(5717) (2005): 1865.

15. Epstein, S.L., et al. DNA vaccine expressing conserved influenza virus proteins protective against H5N1 challenge infection in mice. *Emerging Infectious Diseases* 8(8) (2002): 796–801.

16. Guan, Y., et al. H5N1 influenza viruses isolated from geese in Southeastern China: Evidence for genetic reassortment and interspecies transmission to ducks. *Virology* 292(1) (2002): 16–23.

17. Hampson, A.W. Pandemic influenza: History, extent of the problem and approaches to control. *Developments in Biologicals* (Basel) 110 (2002): 115–23.

18. Hampton, T. Clues to the deadly 1918 flu revealed. *Journal of the American Medical Association* 291(13) (2004): 1553.

19. Hastings, M. and F. Guterl. Bird-flu challenge. *Newsweek* 144(23) (2004): 67.

20. Hatta, M. and Y. Kawaoka. The continued pandemic threat posed by avian influenza viruses in Hong Kong. *Trends in Microbiology* 10(7) (2002): 340–4.

21. Hien, T.T., M. de Jong, and J. Farrar. Avian influenza—a challenge to global health care structures. *New England Journal of Medicine* 351(23) (2004): 2363–5.

22. Kuiken, T., et al. Avian H5N1 influenza in cats. *Science* 306(5694) (2004): 241.

23. Li, K.S., et al. Genesis of a highly pathogenic and potentially pandemic H5N1 influenza virus in eastern Asia. *Nature* 430(6996) (2004): 209–13.

24. Monto, A.S. The threat of an avian influenza pandemic. *New England Journal of Medicine* 352(4) (2005): 323–5.

25. Nicholson, K.G., J.M. Wood, and M. Zambon. Influenza. *Lancet* 362(9397) (2003): 1733–45.

# Notes

26. Normile, D. Infectious diseases. Ducks may magnify threat of avian flu virus. *Science* 306(5698) (2004): 953.

27. Parry, J. Hong Kong under WHO spotlight after flu outbreak. *British Medical Journal* 327(7410) (2003): 308.

28. Parry, J. South East Asia sets up task force to tackle avian flu. *British Medical Journal* 329(7471) (2004): 876.

29. Pearson, H. 'Reverse genetics' could offer forward-thinking flu vaccine. *Nature* 426(6968) (2003): 742.

30. Pickrell, J. The 1918 pandemic. Killer flu with a human-pig pedigree? *Science* 292(5519) (2001): 1041.

31. Pilcher, H. Increasing virulence of bird flu threatens mammals. *Nature* 430(6995) (2004): 4.

32. Quirk, M. USA to manufacture two million doses of pandemic flu vaccine. *Lancet Infect. Dis.* 4(11) (2004): 654.

33. Ready, T. Race for pandemic flu vaccine rife with hurdles. *Nature Medicine* 10(3) (2004): 214.

34. Scholtissek, C. Source for influenza pandemics. *European Journal of Epidemiology* 10(4) (1994): 455–8.

35. Shortridge, K.F., J.S. Peiris, and Y. Guan. The next influenza pandemic: lessons from Hong Kong. *Journal of Applied Microbiology* 94 (Suppl.) (2003): 70S–79S.

36. Shute, N. Of birds and men. A deadly virus is brewing in Asia. Could this be the next killer pandemic? *US News & World Report* 138(12) (2005): 40–8.

37. Stephenson, I. Are we ready for pandemic influenza H5N1? *Expert Reviews of Vaccines* 4(2) (2005): 151–5.

38. Taubenberger, J.K., et al. Initial genetic characterization of the 1918 "Spanish" influenza virus. *Science* 275(5307) (1997): 1793–6.

39. Webster, R. and D. Hulse. Controlling avian flu at the source. *Nature* 435(7041) (2005): 415–6.

40. Weiss, R.A. Cross-species infections. *Current Topics in Microbiology and Immunology* 278 (2003): 47–71.

41. Wood, J.M. and R.A. Levandowski. The influenza vaccine licensing process. *Vaccine* 21(16) (2003): 1786–8.

42. Wood, J.M. and J.S. Robertson. From lethal virus to life-saving vaccine: developing inactivated vaccines for pandemic influenza. *Nature Reviews Microbiology* 2(10) (2004): 842–7.

43. Worobey, M., et al. Questioning the evidence for genetic recombination in the 1918 "Spanish flu" virus. *Science* 296(5566) (2002): 211 discussion 211.

44. Zeitlin, G.A. and M.J. Maslow. Avian influenza. *Current Infectious Disease Reports* 7(3) (2005): 193–199.

Barry. John M. *The Great Influenza: The Epic Story of the Deadliest Plague in History.* New York, NY: Viking, 2005.

Knipe, David M., and Howley, Peter M. *Fields Virology.* Philadelphia, PA: Lippincott Williams and Wilkins, 2002.

White, David O., and Fenner, Frank J., *Medical Virology*, San Diego, CA: Academic Press, 1994.

# Websites

Centers for Disease Control and Prevention
**http://www.cdc.gov/flu/**

The World Health Organization
**http://www.who.int/en/**

CNN special report on Cold and Flu
**http://www.cnn.com/SPECIALS/2004/cold.flu/**

The United States federal government Website for information
about the influenza virus
**http://pandemicflu.gov**

All the virology on the world wide web
**http://www.virology.net/garryfavwebindex.html**

The Big Picture Book of Viruses
**http://www.virology.net/Big_Virology/BVHomePage.html**

Morbidity and Mortality Weekly Report
**http://www.cdc.gov/mmwr/index.html**

# Index

1918 pandemic. *See* Spanish flu
1957 pandemic (Asian flu), 11, 13, 50, 54–55
1968 pandemic (Hong Kong flu), 11–12, 13

adaptation, 43–44
adenoviridae, 30
A/Goose/Guangdong/1 /96, 54–55, 58
Alaska, 8–10, 12
amantadine, 41
anthrax, 20–21
antibodies, 32–34, 36, 37
antigenic drift, 36–37, 55–57, 74
antigenic shift, 54, 55,
aquatic birds, 34, 44–46, 56–57, 59
Asian flu, 11, 13, 50, 54–55
attachment, 38, 50–51
A/Vietnam/1203/04, 61

*Bacillus anthracis*, 20–21, 22
beta-propiolactone, 68
binding, 38, 50–51
biosecurity, 53
birds. *See also individual bird types*; waterfowl
glycoproteins and, 50
hemagglutinins and, 39
infection in, 26
viruses of, 14, 33, 60–61
boundary-defining mutations, 36
Brevig, Alaska, 8–10, 12
broods, 45
broths, 21–22

Canada, 45, 46, 62–63
capsid, 25, 30, 32
capsid proteins, 31, 32
capsules, 24
cats, 62–63
Centers for Disease Control and Prevention (CDC), 14, 16, 69–71, 73–74
chickens, 26, 56, 58, 61
children, 15
China, 46–53, 56–57, 60, 62–63, 65, 67
cholesterol, 32
classification, 32–34
conformational changes, 52–53
contagiousness, 22
contamination, 17–18, 74
cores, 30
criteria for pandemic generation, 14–15, 27–28
cross-species reassortment, 54–55
culling, 66–67
culture media, 19, 21–22

date of isolation, 39–41
deaths. *See* mortality statistics
deoxyribonucleic acid (DNA), 30
detergents, 68
dilutions, 19
diseases, 19–22
disinfection, 65–66
diversity, 37, 38
domesticated birds, 26–27
drift, 36–37, 55–57, 74
drugs, 41. *See also* vaccines
ducks, 26, 45–48, 50, 54–55, 56, 57, 58, 64, 65, 67

ecological niches, 43
economic impacts, 48–49, 65–66
eggs, 48–49, 68, 70–71, 74–75
electron microscopy, 25, 27, 35
encapsulation, 32
entry, 29–31, 52–53
envelopes, 30
epidemics, 33. *See also individual epidemic names*; pandemics
epitopes, 36

fatalities. *See* mortality statistics
fatty layer, 25
fecal-to-oral transmission, 45–46
fermentation, 17
fibers, 30
filtration, 21–22
flasks, 17–18
flocks, 45–46
formalin, 68
fowl. *See* birds; waterfowl
fusion peptides, 38, 52–53

geese, 45–48, 50, 56–58, 64, 65
gelatin, 19, 21
genetic material, 24, 74
genomes, 31
geography, 39–41
glycoproteins. *See also* hemagglutinins; neuraminidases
defined, 37
function of, 37–38
H2N2 virus and, 54–55
species specificity and, 50
structure and, 30, 31–32
vaccines and, 68–69

# Index

# Index

# About the Author

**Jeffrey N. Sfakianos** Ph.D. was trained as a virologist in the Department of Microbiology at the University of Alabama at Birmingham. Currently, he is a postdoctoral fellow in the Department of Cell Biology at Yale University, where he studies epithelial cell morphology and protein sorting. He has authored and coauthored more than 10 peer-reviewed manuscripts in the fields of virology, pharmacology, and cell biology. His hobbies include designing computer graphic animations of scientific mechanisms, such as assembly of virus capsids and drug-binding behaviors. Additionally, he enjoys riding mountain bikes and hiking with his wife, who is also a postdoctoral fellow at Yale University; his son, Alexander; and their black Labrador retriever, Cricks. They all live in Connecticut.

# About the Founding Editor

The late **I. Edward Alcamo** was a Distinguished Teaching Professor of Microbiology at the State University of New York at Farmingdale. Alcamo studied biology at Iona College in New York and earned his M.S. and Ph.D. degrees in microbiology at St. John's University, also in New York. He had taught at Farmingdale for over 30 years. In 2000, Alcamo won the Carski Award for Distinguished Teaching in Microbiology, the highest honor for microbiology teachers in the United States. He was a member of the American Society for Microbiology, the National Association of Biology Teachers, and the American Medical Writers Association. Alcamo authored numerous books on the subjects of microbiology, AIDS, and DNA technology as well as the award-winning textbook *Fundamentals of Microbiology*, now in its sixth edition.